STORIES FROM THE
MANAGER'S OFFICE

STORIES FROM THE MANAGER'S OFFICE

Hermann Jakob Dorner
HOTEL MANAGER

ATHENA PRESS
LONDON

STORIES FROM THE MANAGER'S OFFICE
Copyright © Hermann Jakob Dorner 2010

ISBN 978 1 84748 801 5

First published 2010 by
ATHENA PRESS
Queen's House, 2 Holly Road
Twickenham TW1 4EG
United Kingdom

Printed for Athena Press

Prologue

'Well, my son,' said my father about a year before my leaving school, 'what are your thoughts for the future?'

The answer to the question was quite easy as I had made my decision sometime before to become a cook.

So in 1943 I started my career in the hotel industry as an apprentice cook, although things were a little tough in Switzerland. Though not involved in the war, we had strict rationing and catering was controlled by stringent government regulations.

I recall we had two or three meatless days a week, but that did not stop us serving Welsh rarebit where a piece of steak replaced the bread.

The two and a half years of apprenticeship passed quickly and I passed my examination with flying colours.

Being ambitious, I decided to climb the ladder and aim to become a hotel manager, making my way through the ranks. So after a few years in the kitchen, I took up waiting, went to England for a year to learn English and held positions in Switzerland and the Channel Islands as a waiter.

During a summer season as cook in a hotel in Lugano, I met a charming English girl, which ended in a marriage in 1951.

Having moved to England, I embarked on my career as manager, as I was not blessed with enough funds to attend expensive hotel schools.

Chapter One

Shortly after our honeymoon, I started looking around for a suitable position and as we wanted to be together, we pursued an offer of joint management with a large brewery company in Reading and started in a small hotel in Staines on the River Thames. We worked long hours and were given a thorough training in the licensing trade. We were provided with board and lodging and a salary of £2 per person per week. Not much to shout about but being newly married, money matters did not bother us very much. We had a comfortable room overlooking the river, worked similar hours and were content.

Still striving for bigger things, we went job-hunting again after a while and soon enough an opportunity as assistant manager in a famous spa near Birmingham offered itself and off we went. Renting a small bedsitter in the town, I pursued my ambition at the hotel and my wife took a job with a commercial firm, with more responsibilities and more interesting work than in her previous job.

I settled in very quickly. I was given valuable advice that I have never forgotten, when my manager called me into his office one day. After the usual complimentary remarks about my satisfactory performance, he advised me to adapt myself to the English way of life and drop my somewhat dictatorial Swiss German approach to handling staff for the more diplomatic way of the English. Point taken. It is funny, when I think back, even my wife was occasionally in tears at the harsh tone in which I sometimes spoke to her. All this made a good impression on me and I have ever since taken the advice of my manager. I have never regretted this and it has helped me a great deal in the future years.

So after an eventful year or so, we decided to move along. Still not really knowing which path to pursue as far as hotel management was concerned, we ended up as joint managers of a small hotel in the countryside of the Isle of Man. A delightful place, it was actually a country mansion turned into a hotel. We had quite a busy summer season and one or two old characters staying rather permanently at the hotel. One of them was a pilot with a local airline, who had previously been all over the Middle East.

Apart from being mostly the last customer in the bar, he used to go to his room to write furious letters to the company he worked for, only to tear them up again the next morning. He owned an old Jaguar, which was the most precious possession of his life, and he used to spend hours cleaning it. One of his favourite jokes, when he was flying, was to open the cockpit window before takeoff and with a loud voice which could be heard by all passengers in the cabin enquire from the ground crew how to fly 'this thing'.

The other character in this country mansion was an elderly lady who was very fond of rice pudding. The chef was just not able to cook it to her satisfaction. Not a single day passed when I was not called to the dining room to listen to her complaints. However, after some time the complaining ceased and I went to the chef to find out the secret behind this. He opened the cold room and showed me a large bowl with pre-cooked rice pudding, which was covered with green mould on the top. Every day he just collected enough pudding to warm and it was served to the lady in question. Needless to say, I asked him to remove the mould, but to carry on using the pre-cooked rice pudding, which according to him was already three weeks old.

It was also here that I learned to drive, taking the hotel van, without an experienced driver and me with no previous experience. I used to drive up and down the winding country lanes, not without some precarious and sometimes hair-raising situations, but believe it or not, I passed my driving test the first time.

As the hotel was closing for the winter, it was time again to move on. It was back to England and London as assistant night manager in a 700-bedroom hotel. To ease our financial position, we moved in with my wife's parents.

So off I went every night to the West End to quite an interesting way of life. I never visualised that working at night could be so varied and funny at times.

Moral standards still played a big part in hotel policy and were still strictly enforced. There was no such thing as two unmarried persons sharing a room, or a single room being occupied by two people. Our biggest problem was keeping out ladies of the night and this kept us fairly occupied.

My superior was a likable guy but he just hated those ladies and was after them like a hawk its prey. Most of the time they were involved in a shouting match where four-letter words flew around like flies. Many times it was amazing free entertainment for guests relaxing in the hotel lobby. I was getting used to all the tricks of the trade and the ways the women tried to beat the system to get to the rooms and earn some money at the hotel's expense. One of their favourite tricks to gain access to the room was getting the key from the occupant and entering the hotel beforehand. Of course, we were familiar with this approach and it usually ended in failure.

To break the monotony of the normal routine we sometimes relaxed the rules and let a girl proceed to a room. After about ten minutes, once she had been joined by the occupant of the room, we pounced on them. First, we made contact by phone, stating that we believed there was an unauthorised visitor in the room, which was usually denied. We then informed the client that we would personally investigate. Unbeknown to the guest, we had a key that unlocked any lock that was double locked. Needless to say, it was quite a surprise to the people in rooms when, after first knocking on the door, we stood in front of the bed after we told them we were entering. A bit cruel but then they asked for it – they had been forewarned and we had a little diversion from the long night hours.

We also dealt with guests arriving back roaring drunk who had to be taken to their rooms and put to bed. Then there were the ones who liked to spend the night in the hotel lobby. The lady in Room 1001 had trouble getting her dress off and required someone to release the zip at the back, or others who wanted the night waiter to share the bed with them for an hour or two instead of looking after other clients.

So, life went on. This new working routine did, of course, interfere with our personal lives. The only time I saw Mavis, my wife, was for a few hours in the evening and as my rest days usually fell on weekdays, we did not see much of each other.

Also, realising that this kind of work was not helping me much going forward, I joined a hotel in Birmingham as assistant manager. The manager was Swiss like myself, took me under his wing and was a valuable teacher to me. He was thorough, tough and fair. He got excited very easily and broke so many phones that the telephone department wouldn't replace them any more. His apartment was opposite the local newspaper offices and on Sunday afternoons when the Salvation Army band played below in the street, the journalists would send down money to ask the band to move on, which was then taken. This was followed by another note or two from the manager with the request that they carry on playing. I am sure the Salvation Army must have caught on because they returned regularly every Sunday; one way to keep money coming in, I suppose!

The hotel in a way was self-sufficient. We had our own water well a hundred feet below ground and produced our own electricity. We bottled our own Guinness and Bass beer all by hand. One day, a barrel of Bass was ready for bottling and at the same time the cellar man reported sick. Instructed by the manager to carry out this task despite never having done it before, I had no other choice than to go ahead. I had seen the cellar man sucking on a piece of pipe to get the beer flowing, which was then attached to a gadget to which six bottles could be attached. Being ignorant of the procedure, I swallowed the beer, which I sucked through the pipe, with the result I was running to the toilet for the next twenty-four hours.

I was also in Birmingham when my wife told me I was going to be a father soon. Although I was thrilled, I was somewhat worried because in those days employees were not happy to employ assistant managers with family ties. This has now completely changed and brought about a more stabilised atmosphere.

Right from my early schooldays I always wanted to see the world and as Mavis had no objection, we kept our eyes open for a job abroad. Reading an advertisement for a position in Southern Rhodesia (Zimbabwe today) I promptly submitted my application, which was accepted.

Chapter Two

Zimbabwe

The necessary forms had been completed and we were off to Africa. To save money we were booked on the British Overseas Sky Coach flight, which would take four days to reach Salisbury. We left London on a sunny day on-board a Viking aircraft, stopped for lunch and refuelling in Marseilles and stopped overnight in Algiers. There was some shooting going on in the evening so everybody stayed put in the hotel.

The next day after an early breakfast, we were handed a packet lunch and were off for Kano in Nigeria. Lunchtime found us sitting somewhere in the middle of the Sahara outside an airport building in blazing sun and heat. The runway was just a strip of desert sand. We opened our lunch boxes and were immediately attacked by thousands of flies. The food was covered black with them, but who cared. No wonder that about an hour after takeoff most people were airsick. It was very hot in the plane and we were glad to arrive in Kano in the early evening. After supper, some of us ventured into town and we had our first glance of Africa. Somebody must have been listening to the BBC as the boom-boom signal could be heard clearly.

After a good night's rest under mosquito nets we were in the air again and heading for Brazzaville in the Congo. That night a few of us visited a local nightclub for a few drinks. The next day we arrived in Salisbury.

The Highlands Park Hotel was situated just a few miles outside Salisbury; about forty rooms, a bar and a restaurant with weekly dinner dance and film evenings. The staff lived a short distance from the hotel in a small native village consisting of round straw huts. I must say, they kept it clean and tidy.

Mavis and I settled in quite quickly and occupied a nice house with a swimming pool at the back. Our son was born in November and the African climate seemed to suit him.

Of course, managing a hotel in Africa needs some fundamental adjustments on the part of the management. The staff were willing but of course they lacked the experience and training of their counterparts in Europe.

They needed constant supervision and coaching. Twopence, one of the cooks, prepared a perfectly good steak and kidney pie, most times, but then suddenly he would make a complete balls up of the dish. Tennis, the waiter, served two steaks per person during a banquet, causing quite an upset for the kitchen, as they ran out of steak. The cooks, if you did not watch them, would grill about eighty to ninety steaks in advance at 6 p.m. for serving between 8 p.m. and 10 p.m. Don't ever ask for underdone steak because the one you are going to get is probably dry as a bone.

All the Europeans around the hotel were given names by the natives. Mine was Boss Tanga-Tanga and the dog, a black Labrador, was Boss Molee Tanga-Tanga.

One Sunday morning, just a few weeks after we arrived, Mavis came to ask me if the staff could have the Salvation Army come to visit their village. Not to appear a spoilsport, I consented, but regretted it afterwards because most of the staff appeared at work rolling drunk.

To keep down the snakes around the hotel, we offered a reward for every dead snake the staff brought along. I am still convinced the blighters must have had a snake pit somewhere because I just could not believe there were so many snakes around.

In a way, I grew quite fond of the staff, learning never to shout but if necessary explain to them umpteen times how to carry out a task without losing patience. You had to be firm but fair, close an eye and pretend not to notice and look at things from the funny side. What are you going to do when somebody comes along complaining of headache and wants to see a doctor? You send him off with a note to the next clinic and he does not turn up for four days. When questioned after his return, he quite happily tells you the reasons for not turning up.

'On the first day I went to the clinic but it was already closed for the day. The next day I slept a bit longer than usual, stood in the queue and again could not see the doctor. So on the third I really made an effort and did see the doctor, who gave me some pills.'

So far, so good.

I now asked him if he still had the headache when he woke up the first morning.

'Oh no, it was gone.'

'Why the hell didn't you come to work then, the same day?'

'Because I had a headache and had to see the doctor.'

There was quite a bit of petty thieving going on. So to keep it at an acceptable level I used to take the offender to the local police station for punishment, which consisted of sleeping in a cell for two nights on a bread-and-water diet and cleaning motorbikes with a toothbrush. This proved very effective and helped to maintain order and discipline.

Having always had a keen interest in learning more of the customs and traditions of the countries I worked in, I used to lose little time in finding out more about them. So I discovered that if a young man of the local tribe found a girl he wanted to marry, he went to her father to discuss the marriage price. Depending on how wealthy the young man was, the price maybe consisted of one cow, a sack of mealy meal flour, a winter coat, two pairs of socks and a hat.

Now here comes the other part of the deal. If after six months of living together the girl has not become pregnant, he can take the girl back to the father and get his goods back again. Not a bad arrangement.

Now that we were climbing up the ladder, we bought our first car: not a new model but a good second-hand Ford. A car in this part of the world is not really a luxury but a necessity. However, now that we were mobile, we could go and see the country at large. We drove to Inyanga, near Umtali, which was in the highlands of Rhodesia. The roads outside Salisbury were a bit tricky and consisted of two strips of asphalt, rather like a railway track. You had to be careful not to come off them at speed, otherwise you could end up upside down in your car. It nearly happened to us, but luckily we ended up looking the way we had just passed. So now we drove more carefully on such roads.

Our first holidays we spent in Beira in Portuguese East Africa (Mozambique) and in the Gorongoza Game Park. As you were not allowed to enter the park property without a guide, we were astounded to see plenty of game. Beira was quite nice with a fine beach and plenty of seaside restaurants and cafés. There were no locks on our bedroom door and when we wanted to know why, we were told there were no thieves in Beira. I could quite believe this, as the natives were kept quite strict. I watched a policeman slapping a learner driver in the face because he made a mistake. Quite unnecessary, I thought.

Our son was doing fine and had a first-class guardian in our dog. Even the doctor couldn't go near the baby when the dog was around. Time passed quickly and life was pleasant.

I decided the time had come after nearly two years to move on. So there we were again, making plans for where our next destination was going to be.

Chapter Three

Uganda

Uganda was to be our next port of call.

We arrived in Entebbe after an uneventful journey from Rhodesia and were taken to the Lake Victoria Hotel by the chairman of the hotel company for a briefing and an overnight stop.

The next day we left for Mbale at the foot of Mount Elgon to take up residence and the management of the Mount Elgon Hotel. Mbale, the third largest town in Uganda, had a sizable expatriate community consisting mostly of civil service personnel. Local commerce was in the hands of the Asians, who ran all the shops in town. You had to watch them as some had a great tendency to overcharge.

The European Club was the focal point for the expatriates' sports, consisting of a clubhouse with a bar, swimming pool, tennis and squash courts as well as a golf course, and it provided a meeting place for the various clubs and social activities. Although on the surface and at the first glance everything looked all right, you soon felt the typical British colonial attitude. People moved in small groups, and did not easily mix with people above or below their status. We commercials were about at the bottom of the ladder, but as I said, on the whole there was a sense of belonging.

As the hotel and club were the only places in town where there was a bit of life and entertainment for the expatriates, we did quite good business. Our rooms were mostly occupied by European company representatives who visited the town on a regular basis, which of course was a great attraction for the locals, as they did not meet or see new faces around often.

The hotel was new and we settled in quite quickly. We occupied a small bungalow next to the hotel. On warm and quiet nights, we sat on the veranda, enjoyed a drink and listened to the native drums, somewhere in the bush.

We employed an *ayah* to look after our son during the day and he started chatting away in Swahili. Most afternoons you see all the *ayah*s and the children under a large tree not far from the hotel, where he must have picked up the language.

The staff, mostly Africans, were a likeable bunch, but had no or only a little education. They were up to their usual tricks and had to be coached and watched all the time. The chef, a Goan, was doing a good job and we had a good reputation for our food throughout Uganda. Our supplies came mostly from Kenya. We bought vegetables and some poultry from local farmers though.

Once, when I questioned the chef about purchasing live turkeys from them, which as far as I knew could be dying of old age, he assured me that his turkeys would always be tender. I must confess, he proved right every time. His approach was quite simple: put the turkey in a pen, feed it properly for about ten days, then put it on a three-day vinegar and water diet and you would have a tender bird. To make puff pastry, he mixed the flour with butter and avocado pear with very good results. The local fish, which was available already filleted, was placed in the hot oven together with green grass, which produced quite a bit of smoke, adding to the flavour and taste of the fish. This was featured on the menu as 'Smoked Tilapia'.

The only other hotel, which was no competition, was in the next town. The food it served was not too good and the hotel had earned itself the name 'The Dysentery Arms'. Uganda, of course, was not so far developed as Rhodesia and many areas were still unspoiled by European influence.

There was Karamoja where men walked around in their birthday suits and women wore a small apron to cover their sexual parts.

A regular customer in the bar whenever he was in town was Harry, the agriculture officer of this area.

'Why don't you come and spend a weekend with me at my place if you get the time?' he asked, so we arranged a date and I arrived at his place on an early Saturday afternoon. He was not at home, so I made myself comfortable in his living room rondavel. I might explain that his accommodation consisted of three rondavels (round corrugated metal buildings) arranged in a circle with a small green lawn in the middle. One of the rondavels was his bedroom, the other the living room and the third his kitchen.

After helping myself to a drink, he returned in his Land Rover towards the evening with a small oribi buck for supper.

'I thought this was a protected area,' I said to Harry, 'and killing of animals was prohibited.'

'What do you mean? I didn't shoot the beast – it charged my vehicle,' he replied laughing.

We got a fire going and started roasting the meat. The sun was just about setting when we heard some native voices approaching.

'Now then, here comes my nightly cabaret,' he explained. 'This is something you will enjoy.'

Within minutes the place was surrounded with native women starting to sing and move around in a circle. Every so often they turned towards us, lifting their little aprons to expose their sexual parts. This went on for about fifteen minutes, during which time we made jokes about it.

'What the hell was that in aid of?' I asked.

'Quite simple,' Harry explained. 'It has not been raining for the last month or so and they blame me. So they send the womenfolk around to demonstrate their feelings, as the lifting of the apron is an insult to man in their tribal custom. For me it brings variety into my lonely life.'

The next day we went for a ride around the countryside. On leaving I spotted two loaded rifles standing against the wall in the living room.

'Hey, what about those things there?'

'Oh, don't worry; nobody will steal them. But if you left a cow unattended for a minute, it would be gone before you could say "puff",' he replied. 'What can a native do with a rifle? A cow, however, is worth something to him, because his wealth is measured by how many cows he owns.'

Whenever we stopped near a village we were immediately surrounded by a lot of women, old men and children. They all wanted to have a look at themselves in the car mirror. The few men we met on the track had splendid bodies and postures and were a match to any white man. Not surprisingly, you did not take your wife to Karamoja.

Another regular in the bar told me stories of circumcisions in the area. As I was a keen movie photographer, we quickly came to an arrangement for me to take some film. Not long after, we were off into the bush where male circumcisions were taking place. After about an hour's drive we arrived at a village that was teeming with natives, all dancing to wild drums. In no time we were invited to partake in the celebrations.

There we were, dancing in the middle of a very excited crowd, breasts flying all over the place, with heavy body odour coming from the sweating bodies. The young boys to be circumcised were carried shoulder high and seemed to be in a trance. I was told they had been dancing all night.

About lunchtime the party broke up and the people made their way to their homes, where the circumcisions would take place. We followed one of them and after a while the executioner of the circumcision pulled out a knife from his belt, washed his hands and knife in cold water, pulled the skin over the private part and cut it off. He didn't seem to be satisfied with his work, so he trimmed off some more skin, stopped the little bleeding there was with some soil he picked up from the ground and was off on his next call of duty. Tribal custom forbade the young man being circumcised to show any pain or emotion. I doubted if I could do this.

Anyway, I was filming away like mad and it was only when I saw my work that I felt the full impact of the gruesome event. Don't ask me how, but the whole country must have known about my film because more and more visitors to the hotel wanted to see it. The trouble was, I didn't know when to show it. If it was before dinner, it put them off the meal; if I showed it afterwards, they might be sick. Usually I decided to show it after dinner, so I wouldn't lose revenue from food.

By now we belonged to the community and being the hotel manager made you popular. First of all, you always had the latest news and scandal in town and secondly a hotel always creates a certain attraction for people. We had three dogs and a cat at home. Bernard, our son, was going to the kindergarten and sometimes made a nuisance of himself. The Africans on a whole were very fond of children and he was spoilt by them. I had given up telling them not to be bossed around by the little fellow, but without result.

Of course, as everywhere, we had our characters in town. There was the small contractor building a toilet for his staff on his premises. He instructed his workers to dig a hole and went off for a week, only to find that he had a toilet with a twenty-foot hole. One consolation was that it would take a long time until he needed to worry about building a new toilet.

There was Joy, known to the boys as Oh Be Joyful, a girl known for her sexual adventures. Unfortunately, she had a nervous disposition, which made her head shake. All the fellows in the bar wanted to know if she also shook her head when she had somebody in bed with her.

There was another story flying about regarding the local public works road supervisor with a glass eye. Apparently, every time he had his lunch break, he placed his glass eye on a stone overlooking the work area and told his work gang that he was watching them work while he was away. Everything went OK until one day when he found the workers sitting in the shade and found his eye covered with a hat.

Also there was the story (which was quite true) of the married couple who got on remarkably well with each other, but despite this she liked to have a change occasionally. Anyway, the rumour went around that she was pregnant and of course everybody started guessing who the father was and this guessing game was quite a serious debate in the bar, until one day her husband came along, grinning from ear to ear, shouting, 'Boys, it's a false alarm.'

Christmas was like everywhere else in the world, the time where you give gifts to customers and clients alike. This was also the case here. There were quite a number of parcels delivered to the hotel. Their contents were usually shared out to the staff, with the exception of personal gifts.

During my daily discussions with the chef, he said, 'You know one of our major suppliers never brought along a present – although we cannot demand something from him, we should do something about it.'

'How about instead of signing our name for the daily deliveries, why don't we just write "Happy New Year"?' I replied, so for the next month and a half we did just that, and in about the middle of February, a large parcel arrived and we reverted back to signing properly.

In a way, Asian businesses also used the Christmas period to pay back favours received during the year. So when a lot of parcels started to arrive at the vehicle inspector's residence, his neighbour replaced his nameplate in front of the house with that of the inspector's and channelled some of the gifts to his house. Needless to say, after that the two parties were not on speaking terms.

For our holiday, we decided to take in Mombasa at a seaside hotel, with a short trip to Zanzibar. So one evening we found ourselves boarding the overnight express train at Tororo with a through coach to Mombasa. The compartment has couchettes and as we had already had dinner before we left the hotel, we went straight to sleep. On awakening, we were in the highlands of Kenya. The train did not travel very fast, which gave us plenty of time to look at the changing countryside, after a good breakfast in the dining car, which we had to reach by passing through coaches occupied by Asians busy cooking their breakfast on paraffin cookers in the corridors and compartments. The air was full of spicy Indian smells, which were quite acceptable most of the time, but first thing in the morning with an empty stomach, they were not very welcome.

On our return, we found our compartment arranged into a pleasant resting place. As it got warmer outside, the atmosphere got very sticky in the coach and we were glad that the evening brought along a cooler environment. A short stop in Nairobi and we were off on our second night on the train to Mombasa. We passed through Nairobi Game Park and saw some game grazing along the track. They must have become used to the trains passing by because they kept on grazing without the slightest notice.

Early next morning we arrived in Mombasa and a short ride by taxi brought us to the hotel. We were accommodated in small bungalows and settled in quite nicely. Although there was not much beach in front of the hotel, we could walk out to the coral reef when the tide was out. The nights were warm and we decided one evening to sit by the sea and look at the stars. We, however, did not take into consideration the small mosquitoes, which did not give us any peace and nipped away at the uncovered parts of our bodies. Bernie developed prickly heat, which made him a bit irritable.

Not far away from the hotel was a beautiful white sandy beach and we went there quite often to swim and get suntanned. There were not many tourists around and life was very quiet and peaceful.

Next on our itinerary was Zanzibar and we were immediately fascinated by the quaintness of the place. The hotel was situated in the middle of the town. The taxi ride was an experience in its own right. The roads were very narrow and twisty, and the taxi driver had not only to navigate through all this, but also had to watch he was not knocking down any pedestrians. The hotel was many years old – don't ask me how they managed to keep it in such good shape.

We wandered out of the hotel in the late afternoon to have a look around and engaged the services of a guide. I doubted that we could have found our own way in that maze of small alleyways. The air was full of exotic perfumes from tropical plants and flowers. The shops were open until late in the evening and were mostly lit by paraffin lamps, which gave the whole picture a somewhat romantic style.

The next day we rented a taxi to take us around the island. We passed the palace of the Sultan, with the colourful guard in front. We visited the Persian steam baths, various plantations growing sweet smelling plants and bushes for perfume manufacturers and whole acres of clove bushes. We stopped at the old slave market and had a cup of tea on one of the Arab dhows in the old harbour. What an unforgettable sight; the colourful crews from all parts of the Indian Ocean, the Arab dealers in their robes with curved knives in their belts, the chanting of the crews when performing their various duties were things we would not soon forget.

The time passed much too quickly and before we knew it, we were back home again. My three-year assignment was coming to a close and I was asked by the company if I would like to return and take over the Lake Victoria Hotel in Entebbe, the largest hotel in the country. Of course, I jumped at the opportunity and signed a new contract for another three years.

Just before proceeding on overseas leave, I fell ill and had to have my appendix removed. No big sweat: only five weeks in hospital. Mavis and Bernie had already left to go to England, so I was on my own. Not that I lacked visitors – far from it. I must have given my barman a real fright, what with a stomach pump and a drip attached to me. He went straight back to the hotel, telling the guests that I would not make it.

Admittedly, I was in a lot of pain, as the operation wound turned septic. Once the doctor cured that problem, the wound would not heal. I gave them hell every day, complaining and making myself a general nuisance, so the doctor agreed to let me proceed on leave with my stitches, which could be removed in England. After three or four days in England, my wound was closed and the stitches taken out.

We rented a car for the duration of our leave and visited our families in England and Switzerland.

As manager of a small hotel, you were also involved with personnel and welfare matters. So it was not surprising that staff members came to see me with their problems. The same also applied for first aid and small illnesses such as constipation, headaches, cuts and black eyes from fights and so on.

Sometimes their complaints were genuine, other times put on to get time off without losing pay.

Constipation was quite a common complaint and I was at a loss to find a cure. So I contacted the local chemist, who handed me some special pills. So every time someone complained they had not been to the toilet for days, they were handed two or three of these pills. I must say they did the trick. Not only would I not see the person for two or three days, but when they appeared again, they would look rather pale and drawn. When I inquired about his or her state of health, he or she usually confirmed they were cured but were feeling weak as, for the next hours after taking the pills, they were running into the bush every half hour or so.

Strange, but afterwards complaints for these illnesses were cut drastically and most of the time I had to deal with only real cases.

Another favourable trick to get a day off without deduction of pay was to pretend to have some kind of sickness. Mostly very bad headaches. It was no use trying to offer painkillers, which was quite understandable, as they would rather stay at home. It took me quite a while to get to the bottom of the usual complaint, so I devised a simple but effective method, which usually went like this.

A waiter, for instance, would enter my office and stand in front of my desk, holding his head in both his hands and looking very down.

After inquiring the cause of the visit, he would inform me that he had a very bad headache and would like to go home and rest. Naturally, I would be very sympathetic to his pain and ask him whether, if he turned his head to the right, the pain rolls over there, just as if a ball is in his head. (If he turns his head to the left the ball rolls over there and it is very painful.)

By this time he would actually be making the movements with his head and moaning and groaning. Now would arrive the moment of the cure.

'Go back to bloody work,' I would shout as loudly as possible.

He would then wake up from his comedy, and with a 'Yes, sir' go back to work.

You would imagine that in a small town such as Mbale life could be without much excitement and without very much going on. Far from it.

There was the local club, with a swimming pool, tennis courts, squash courts and a golf course. There were the various societies and events, such as the Caledonian Club, St George's Day and Burns Night. Other organisations connected to the club included the Scottish country-dancing club. The only drawback to the whole affair was that you always met the same people whenever you attended a function or meeting.

It was quite a change, then, when a VIP visited the town and was accommodated at the hotel.

At one time, the Aga Khan was staying with us and the local Ismailly community decided to hold a large banquet. Some of my senior staff asked me if they could serve the Aga Khan's party, to which I had no objection. However, on the evening in question, the special waiters were shaking so much as they served the main course that I personally had to take over and serve the VIP party to avoid having the meat and vegetables ending up in their laps.

A few days or so after the party's departure, I discovered a room attendant with a number of bottles filled with water leaving the hotel. On demanding what he was intending to do with the bottles and their contents, he confessed after a lot of questioning that he was selling the Aga Khan's bath water in town. I had quite a laugh to myself and let him proceed, making a few shillings on the side.

Being a hotel manager in a small town automatically makes you an important person, in line with the local doctor or bank manager.

Also, as a manager, you are required to do a bit of public relations for the hotel and the way to do this is to join the various clubs and institutions that exist in town. Mavis was also part and parcel of this and we both belonged to organisations and clubs. One thing, however, I couldn't do was take over a function on the committee as I had enough work at the hotel without being burdened with doing committee work. Some clubs were multiracial; others were reserved only for Europeans.

The Round Table, which met regularly at the hotel, like all other multiracial clubs, had quite a considerable number of Asian members. I must say, they were very interested in club matters and didn't miss many meetings or other social gatherings. It must be remembered that some Asians, and Africans for that matter, have a very good knowledge of English and this manifested itself during speeches that were given by them. I recall during a farewell dinner for the provincial governor that one of Indian members mentioned during the speech that the governor was a very sympathetic man, always finding time to discuss a particular subject or problem with everyone; in other words, 'he was just like a public convenience'.

On another occasion, a certain member was praised for having very good business connections and having a finger in every pie, but what the speaker actually said was, 'that he was having a finger in every tart'. Serious faces all round, but with a faint smile on some faces at the table.

Chapter Four

Relaxed and fully recovered, we returned to Uganda once more.

Entebbe, apart from being the location of the international airport, was also the administration centre of the British colonial government and about twenty miles from Kampala, the commercial and main town of the country.

Our clients were mostly tourists, people proceeding on or returning from leave and some aircrews stopping over.

We collected our animals, which we boarded out during our holidays, and settled down again. There was a lot of talking and speculating going on as Uhuru (Independence) was just around the corner. Mavis and I took up golf and Bernie started school in earnest. There was a lot of social life around, with a lot of scandal attached to it. As the hotel catered for most of the parties, I heard quite interesting stories from my staff as to what was going on.

As I mentioned earlier, we had a number of aircrews staying at the hotel, and although they were on the whole quite well behaved, they could be troublesome, especially after a few drinks late in the bar. Swinging from curtains was one of their favourite games, or removing shoes that had been placed outside the rooms for cleaning to another place. I then had the pleasure in the morning of trying to calm down clients looking for their shoes and tour guides complaining of being late for their tour schedule.

Naturally, the hostesses were a good attraction for the local bachelors, but they usually barked up the wrong tree, as the girls, after being wined and dined, would bugger off with the male members of the crew.

The tourists were no problem whatsoever. They were usually so tired from seeing the country and the wildlife that they disappeared straight to bed after dinner. Mind you, I did not blame them, as they were usually woken up around 5 a.m. in the morning with breakfast at 6 a.m.

Apart from managing the hotel, we catered for most state

functions and state visits. This was not an easy tasks as these functions usually involved outside catering for between 200–800 persons.

I was asked to prepare menus for visiting English royalty for a stay and visits to various parts of the country, for a duration of ten days. Luckily I knew most of the hotels and their capabilities from previous visits. I was handed a list of dishes that should and should not be included in the menus, preference of drinks, cigarettes and so on. After approval of the suggested menus, my next stop was to go and see the various managers involved and discuss the menus with them and place orders for items that are not available in the country and that have to be air freighted. One hurdle that usually caused quite a problem was the customs clearance. But no questions were asked, no complications put in our way and the goods were released without problem.

Another royalty visit involved a two-week safari in the bush. We supplied the camp every four days with fresh food, drinks and clean linen. I personally visited the site on one occasion to see that everything was in order. On arrival, I was questioned by the VIP regarding my presence at the camp.

'I am the man responsible for your well-being, Your Excellence.'

'Cut that out and call me "sir". Sit down and join us for lunch.'

The soup was served and I noticed some dead flies swimming in it. So after the meal I went to see the chef.

'I have been trying to take them out, but on one occasion during the visit to the kitchen by His Excellency I was told not to bother and just serve the soup.'

The chef was quite relaxed and said he thought it was very easy to look after royalty.

Uhuru was fast approaching and the staff were becoming restless. It needed a lot of patience and persuasion to maintain the service and standard of the hotel. Most of them thought that paradise would come after Uhuru – no more hard work and plenty of freedom. Petty thieving was on the increase and we issued strict instructions to the security.

'Sir, can I see you for a minute?' asked a security guard.

'Sure, what's the problem?'

'This man here refuses to be searched.'

'Why don't you want to be searched?' I asked the man.

'I don't object to being searched, but I refuse to take off my trousers in front of all the other staff.'

'OK, security, let him pass and if you have to make a body search, take him to your office.'

Most likely the reason the security man wanted to show the man his authority and his power to enforce the rules was because he did not like him. Probably all his friends passed by with a very minimal check.

The penalty for petty thieving usually involved being taken to the police station for a charge, which in turn was followed by court proceedings at which the manager of the business had to be present. So off I went nearly every week to attend court. The Ugandan magistrate had some sympathy for me and handed down quite a stiff sentence, which helped in a great way to stop thieving.

'Where are you working?' asked the judge.

'Lake Victoria Hotel, sir.'

'What are you accused of?'

'Stealing three eggs, sir.'

'Now, this has to stop. You see your manager sitting there, wasting valuable time, because of you thieving people? Five months' jail for each egg and I hope this will be a lesson to all of you.'

'Yes, thank you, sir.'

Uhuru had come and gone about a week before. The European chef had gone on well-deserved leave and the management was looking after the catering.

We were all still a bit edgy and the kitchen staff were playing up. The food was of poor quality, cold, and the hotel was fully booked and was receiving lots of complaints. So one evening during my term of duty I stormed into the kitchen to give the cook a piece of my mind.

'You get out of this kitchen. We are now free and you can't order us around,' said one of the cooks.

A heavy argument ensued and the only thing I remember is waking up in hospital. Mavis told me that one of the assistant managers informed her that I was found unconscious in the kitchen and taken to hospital. After three days' rest in bed, I returned to the hotel to take up where I left off. Don't ask me why, but after my return and not giving way, matters improved considerably. I had a white coat hanging in the kitchen, which I put on every time I had something to do there. Now, suddenly, someone in the kitchen always helped me to put the coat on and when we left for a short assignment to Europe, the kitchen staff presented me with a set of golden Parker pens, which I still use today. Whether they felt sorry for what happened or they realised that I was a strict manager but always very fair, I don't know.

The hotel catered for quite a large variety of guests. There were those who came and visited the country to see the national parks, the tourist and stopover passengers, aircrews and people arriving in or departing the country.

There was a very large community of Catholic priests deployed in the country. Some of them had quite a rough life, especially if they were stationed in very remote locations. But they were always cheerful and one could always be sure of very hospitable welcomes, a good lunch and a glass or two of whisky when you paid them a visit. Mostly they came from Holland and Ireland. They had a long stint of eight years in Uganda before going back to Europe for twelve months' leave. A chartered aircraft arrived every few months to take the clergy home and bring them back.

The ones that were going assembled at the hotel about two days before departure and could drink and eat to their hearts' content. A local resident told me once to go to the airport and watch the arrival of the returning priests. If you have never seen a crowd of black-clothed clergymen having a ball, doing a highland dance on the tarmac and singing quite questionable songs, then you have missed a good laugh. Having been looked after very well on the aircraft, they were all in a very happy mood and let their feelings run wild. It would be their last fling before the next eight-year tour.

Of course, we also had some delayed or unscheduled stop-overs from time to time.

'Can you accommodate about one hundred Pakistanis on the way back from Mecca for the night?' asked the airport clerk. No problem, send 'em along.

If I had known what was in store for us, I would have sent them to Kampala to another hotel, because not only were they making a general nuisance of themselves, but over 150 bed sheets were missing once they left the hotel. We had wondered, actually, why so many were wearing white turbans when they left the hotel.

Our local holidays were due again and we decided to tour Uganda. As the company owned nearly all the hotels in the country, it turned out to be an inexpensive holiday. We took all the necessary gear required for a long safari as well as our golf clubs and set off for Murchison Falls Game Park. The manager, a cheerful Scot, invited us to go fishing on the Nile. Just having returned from a tour of the river the previous day and having seen a lot of crocodiles basking on the riverbank, Mavis and I were of course somewhat concerned.

'Don't you worry about that! We go fishing just below the waterfall where the current of the river is quite strong and the crocs don't like it there,' was his reply, 'and you will hook some quite big fish around there.'

True enough, we caught about ten eight- to twelve-pound fish within an hour. So that night the guests in the game lodge had freshly grilled Nile perch on the menu. Of course, being a Scot, the manager sold the fish to the hotel at going market price.

One of the attractions in the evening after dinner and sitting on the terrace was to watch an elephant coming along and sorting out the rubbish bins. Empty tins and any other non-edible items were thrown all over the place. Everybody went to bed early and guests returning late for a nightcap in the bar to their chalets had to be careful not to cross the path of elephants strolling along in the area of the lodge.

I was sleeping quite soundly when Mavis woke me because of strange sounds outside. Getting up to have a look through the window, I saw an elephant rubbing his side against the bungalow wall.

What could anybody do about it, other than pray that he did

not use force and make the wall cave in? Anyway, he moved off without any damage caused.

Our next stop was Mbarara to visit some friends and then on to Kabale to the White Horse Inn. A beautiful spot, very lush and green. It was an olde-worlde type of hotel with a nice golf course and fresh crisp air. We were really sorry to leave.

Through the impenetrable forest, we made our way to the Queen Elizabeth Game Park and spent a few days there, driving around the park. Different than Murchison Falls Park, we saw a lot of different game and great flocks of pelicans and other birds. Of course, elephants had the right of way and one of these brutes kept us waiting for nearly an hour before he decided to make way. The Maribu vultures, ugly birds, sat mostly on trees surrounding the lodge kitchen, waiting for scraps. Large herds of buffalo and wildebeest roamed the plains.

Next stop was Fort Portal and we decided to pay the pygmies a visit down in the Congo plains. The road leading there was very narrow and full of the usual potholes. Traffic was one-way going there in the morning and coming back in the afternoon.

Having driven down the escarpment, we arrived after about half an hour on the plain. Driving was better here and we kept a lookout for the pygmies. We must have been past the last trading post about five miles back and were thinking of returning, when suddenly out of the bush about six of them appeared. Sitting on the bonnet of the car, they directed the way through the under-growth to their village. There they were all dressed to kill and to dance. I took out my film camera to take some film, when one of them came along, demanding payment of twenty US dollars. After being paid, they started to perform some of their dances. Before we left, they offered us some souvenirs to buy. I just couldn't get over their sales technique. When I spoke to a local in the bar that evening, he told me that a lot of American tourists go there and of course they are very generous with their greenbacks.

'But what can those pygmies do with all that money? Surely they do not know the value of it?' I asked.

'Quite simple,' he replied, 'the bloke running the trading post is making quite a packet and many times the pygmies bury their money in the ground, only to find that the ants have eaten it.'

Back at home we could look back on a very enjoyable and interesting holiday.

One of the British practises left over before they departed was to introduce trade unionism to the country. Now, don't get me wrong, I have nothing against unions but to try to educate illiterate people to the working of union practices is quite another thing. Because they paid one shilling per month union fee, they were of the opinion that you couldn't dismiss or discipline them and the smallest incident was reported to union officials. He (the official) was not really worried about his members. He received a regular income, had a good life, most likely had a car and felt important. Of course, he had to show that he was concerned about the members' complaints, so he made himself a big nuisance to the management. He was open to bribes, but when things became a bit sticky, he couldn't always back down.

Now the union wanted an increase for all grades of hotel staff, throughout the country. The company refused to pay, so they called a strike at the largest hotel and most profitable in the country, the Lake Victoria Hotel.

Knowing that a strike was unavoidable, we made some plans about how to deal with the situation. Mavis and Bernie went and stayed with friends and some local management staff moved to the hotel. Local European girls and boys ran the bar and served in the restaurant. Some of the aircrew ran the laundry and everything went very smoothly.

A lady from Kenya even called me to her table while having breakfast and said, 'This is about the best holiday I've had for a long time, because I haven't see a black face for days.'

We were sorry in a way when the strike fizzled out after about four days, as we had all had a grand time. But then, of course, the workers had no union money as there was nothing in the kitty and they were forced to return to work to be able to feed their families. Not only did we have the union trying to make their presence felt, occasionally management was even reported to the Prime Minister. So it wasn't a surprise when I was called to his office.

I was shown into the PM's office and asked to sit down. The PM continued reading the newspaper for about five minutes. He turned to me saying he had heard I had made a remark in the kitchen, 'You Africans are all the same: not much good.' Did I realise that this also included him?

I replied that it had never entered my mind or that I even intended to include the Prime Minister in my remark.

The second time I was called to see him was about my housekeeper, a very nice German woman, seventy years of age, a strong disciplinarian and who sometimes under the pressure of work called her staff 'monkeys'. I was fully aware of this and I had spoken to her before on this subject and also explained the circumstances leading up to the incident. Further, I told him it was not always easy to control oneself, especially under stress and when staff made really stupid mistakes, and furthermore it made it very difficult for management to run the hotel when staff could go to the Prime Minister every time a word was uttered. I think this little conversation must have done the trick because during a government function, the PM called me to him.

'Come here, manager,' he said. 'I am still getting complaints about your hotel, but I throw them straight in the paper basket.'

'Thank you, sir,' I replied.

Some African staff were heavy-handed and were quite good at breaking things in no time. A typical example of this was the number of carpet cleaners and polishers that were returned to the maintenance department. The department just could not repair them fast enough before they were back in the workshop again. We just had to find a simple solution to the problem as trying to educate the staff about how to use the appliances proved fruitless. As all our bedrooms had polished floors and the polishers topped the list of items getting broken, we came up with a solution: to hand each room attendant a pair of lambskin pieces which he could slip on his feet, let them switch on the radio in the room and polish the floor to the rhythm of the music. I must say, this answer to the problem was a great success and the housekeeper reported that she had never seen such sparkling floors in all her life.

On taking over the management, I noticed the waiters using trolleys for service in the restaurant. Not only was it time-consuming, it also annoyed the clients because they had to move frequently to allow the waiters to pass. When I saw one of the staff pushing a trolley around with just one plate on it with sardines on toast, I'd had enough. Out went the trolley and the waiters were trained to use trays instead.

What a performance for the first few weeks, especially during busy periods. First of all, it took them days to get past the double doors between the kitchen and restaurant. Invariably they were not fast enough, so the closing door hit the tray they were balancing on one hand, causing plates and food to spill on the floor. By the time everything was cleared, another two or three waiters came crashing through the door and promptly slipped on the wet surface as no shoes were worn. Believe you me, it was frustrating in the beginning and I seriously contemplated giving back the trolleys, but I was happy to note they got the hang of things and everything went smoothly eventually.

After Ugandan independence, Kenya was next in line. To celebrate the birth of a new nation, some of the younger expatriates decided to hold a party under the motto 'The end of the White Man's Burden' in a house in Kampala. Invitations to attend the so-called 'Shrunken Head bottle party' arrived about two or three days before the event and Mavis and I decided to be part of it. Armed with a bottle of booze, we drove to the house and handed over the bottles, which were promptly emptied into a toilet basin standing on a table. Blimey, can you imagine what a concoction that turned out to be? Everybody was in high spirits and after about three glasses I was bombed out of my mind. The only thing I can remember was being violently sick on the way home and Mavis just had to stop and open the door for me, otherwise I would have made a nice mess in the car. That's about all I can remember of the evening.

The next day, being Saturday and just a few days before Christmas, I went to head office in Kampala to settle some outstanding matters. I dropped in at the City Bar to have a drink with friends before returning home and I found some unusual excitement in the place.

'Have you heard about that party, last night?' was the greeting.

'Yes, why, what about it?'

'The police raided the place, took everybody's name and address, and took away a list of all invitees. Apparently some companies have taken precautions already to send some of the participants across the border into Kenya.'

As no one was any the wiser on what steps the government would take, I left for home. By that time, the news had also arrived in Entebbe and the club was full of rumours by the evening and were confirmed the next day. A number of people who were at the party with their wives and children were asked to leave the country within two days and this just a day before Christmas. The house in which the party was held was burned to the ground and the police were rounding up anyone connected with the party.

Mavis and I were awaiting our marching orders within the hour. Sure enough, 10 a.m. that day in December, I had a visit from the chief of police in my office.

'I understand you were at the party two nights ago?'

As they must have had a list of all people invited, there was no point in a denial and I affirmed this question with the remark, 'Just give me twenty-four hours to leave, as I have a lot to pack.'

'Who says you will be given your marching orders?' he replied. 'Just tell me, what is a bottle party?'

I can tell you, I was relieved after that piece of good luck.

Directives from above indicated that hotel management should be more and more Ugandanised, with a number of trainee managers and understudies in each hotel. I had about five of them allocated to me. Strange how quickly they learned to boss around the staff and demand favours from them. It was tough for them because they couldn't go and report the white boss any more, because they were administered by their own people. Instead, they now ran to me with their complaints. Although I listened to them I had to back my managers to a certain extent, which did not help keep the peace with the union officials. So they started breathing down my neck more frequently. One of these young managers had just returned from a year's training in England at a hotel school. He arrived in my office in striped trousers and black jacket, with a white shirt and with a briefcase in his hand. He sat down in a chair and started.

'I don't like the accommodation. Mend the bed linen, and I require a fridge, a kitchenette installed and a TV.'

I did not believe my ears, so I turned on the heat.

'Now you listen to me, young man,' I started. 'To begin with, you can take off this outfit you are wearing: trousers, shirt and tie during the day and jacket in the evening. Now stand up because I never invited you to sit down and as far as your accommodation is concerned, this was and still is of a much higher standard than you have been used to before, so take it or leave it.'

It must have been quite a shock to him, because he turned out to be one of my best and most trustworthy assistants.

Our second tour in Uganda was coming to a close and after six years with no further prospect for climbing any higher, I started looking for something new to get my teeth into.

Chapter Five

Nigeria

We were accommodated with my parents. Bernie was going to school and had quite a problem to adjust himself. He took on the whole class for a fight because they call him *'neger'* – black man – which he very much resented, but otherwise he seemed to be quite happy.

As we hoped to travel abroad again, he was to remain in Switzerland for his schooling, and we visited together with him a number of private schools and decided eventually on Klosters, which was not far from my parents' home.

So, having spent a few weeks' holiday in Switzerland, I boarded the plane at Zurich bound for Lagos and Enugu. I changed planes in Lagos and arrived at Enugu airport, which consisted of a small runway with a prefab ground-floor office building. *Blimey, this looks a bit miserable,* I thought and became even more depressed when the car that collected me at the airport drove through some shantytowns to the hotel.

My fears, however, were unjustified, and I could hardly believe my eyes when I entered the hotel. The spacious lobby was all green marble, dominated by a large wooden sculpture and a fountain with water lilies floating on the water. My apartment, splendidly furnished, had a sunken bath all in mosaic, and a balcony with a splendid view over the countryside. A tour of the hotel made an even bigger impression on me. Within the hotel there was a restaurant, coffee shop, games room and a nightclub with chairs and stools covered with real leopard skin and with the latest audio equipment. Next to this was a cinema with a bar that featured films four nights a week. In addition, the area could also be used as an auditorium for conferences and so on. Outside there was an Olympic-sized swimming pool with changing rooms, cabanas and a restaurant complemented by two all-weather tennis courts. I must say, I was not prepared for anything like this. Unfortunately, the hotel was a bit of a white elephant with a not-too-healthy turnover. But that loss was compensated by the sister hotel in Port Harcourt.

Mavis joined me shortly after, but Bernie stayed behind in Switzerland and started attending school there. We thought it would not be to his advantage changing school too often.

The political climate in Nigeria was not too good and became even more acute, with eastern Nigeria wanting to secede from the rest of Nigeria. Despite warnings from friendly governments, they eventually went ahead with their plan. Anyway, this was still some months off and did not affect our normal daily life. We played a lot of golf, joined the club and made new friends. Having already had experience under African rule, I wasn't surprised to receive phone calls from government officials to send hotel goods to their homes. The hotel laundry washed more linen and personal articles for high-ranking government officials than for hotel guests. Once, driving down to town, I saw some children running around, dressed in the hotel's page uniforms. When making enquiries later on, I was told that they were children of one of the government ministers who had taken a number of uniforms away with him the last time he had visited the hotel laundry.

The manager of the sister hotel left the country after the expiry of his contract and I was asked to transfer there and take over the hotel, while a new man would be appointed for Enugu.

Although the Port Harcourt property was not as luxurious as Enugu, it did fantastic business. It had similar facilities but was larger in size. The European community was large and mostly were employed in the oil-exploration industry. Shell had its own town, where they housed their expatriates. We were desperately short of rooms and were fully booked every day. The restaurant and bars were full all the time and the nightclub open until 4 or 5 a.m. The swimming club had a long waiting list and the money rolled in.

Port Harcourt was growing fast and could not keep up with the developments brought about through the discovery of oil. The telephone system was inadequate and outdated. A local call took up to thirty minutes before you were connected and sometimes one never got through. Overseas calls could take up to twelve hours. The roads were full of potholes, which made driving quite an experience, more so during the rainy season, when the depth of the hole couldn't be seen. Food was plentiful as there were no import restrictions and money seemed to be the least of anyone's problems. Corruption was still widespread, although the military government was very strict in dealing with offenders. The Ibo tribe were very enterprising and shrewd business people. Tribal customs were still very strong and we tried to employ people from many various tribes in the hotel as, in case of a labour dispute or other problems, the effect on business would be minimal, as no one tribe was strong enough to force an issue and cooperation between them was very lax.

The surrounding countryside was lit up by a number of gas fires from the oil fields, which added quite a romantic atmosphere during the evening and night. The road system was improving all the time, but the main road leading to Enugu had a number of dangerous and narrow sections. The lorries were the kings and drove along at us without a care in the world. On one occasion, a pedestrian got knocked unconscious and was believed dead by the fast-gathering crowd, who lynched the driver. They justified their actions when the unlucky pedestrian gained consciousness by also killing him. So in the eyes of the local people, they cleared themselves of any crime.

Our staff had their own taxi service organised, which was run by the owner of a bicycle. The passenger was charged ten cents for a mile, sitting on the luggage and mounted on the back wheel. A fifty per cent discount is offered if the passenger did the pedalling and the owner sat on the back.

However, the storm clouds started to build up very rapidly. We were looking forward to seeing Bernie again, who was expected to spend his holidays with us. But two days before his arrival, war broke out. As a precaution, foreign governments advised the European women and children to leave the country. So after only a few weeks together, Mavis was back in Europe again. The company asked me to take charge of both hotels, so there I was, travelling back and forth every two or three weeks.

Biafra was preparing itself to meet the Nigerian troops in combat. Being very short of military equipment, they improvised wherever they could. Earth-moving equipment became tanks, lorries troop carriers with mounted machine guns. Airplanes confiscated on the day hostilities broke out became war planes and bombers. Young men were trained as soldiers, using sticks in place of guns during exercise. The platoon stationed at the hotel had only one or two old guns, but that soon changed as more and more planes loaded full with weapons arrived nearly every night at Port Harcourt airport. We still had plenty of supplies at both hotels and life went on as normal except there were no white women around.

On one of my returns from Enugu, having passed through about twenty army roadblocks on the way, I found a note waiting for me from a permanent guest. It went as follows:

Dear Hermann,

You do not have to tell me when you leave the hotel for Enugu because it becomes apparent after a day or so, as the service deteriorates. For example, the toilet paper in the bathroom was running out, and despite repeated requests, nothing was done. I am using hotel stationery at the moment and when that is finished I do not know what to do.

Use the shower curtain for the time being, was my reply.

The general situation started hotting up. The country was virtually cut off from the outside world, so the oil companies closed down shop and evacuated all remaining Europeans in Port Harcourt, which was a sign for all remaining others to leave also. The company's chairman asked me to remain and carry on looking after the two hotels. Should things turn worse, they promised to get me out of the country. So I stayed put.

There were only one or two of us left in Enugu and about twenty in Port Harcourt. I still travelled back and forth between Enugu and Port Harcourt. The roadblocks became much stricter; every time I had to open my suitcase and at one time I was over half an hour at a checkpoint because I would not press the button on my transistor radio. The soldier maintained it could be a bomb and would not let me pass before he was certain it was harmless.

My secretary in Enugu was a European girl whose husband had been sent to Lagos for a sabotage mission and was killed. She had two children to look after. The war started getting nearer to Enugu and when, on one of my visits, the rockets started hitting the area around the hotel, I packed my cases and left Enugu for good, along with the secretary and her children.

Port Harcourt was reasonable, apart from the Nigerian navy ships patrolling off shore to enforce the blockade. The only way to get out of Biafra was along the coast to Cameroon with small boats, a hazardous journey that some of the remaining expatriates undertook to get out of Biafra. So in the end we were about six left. The hotel was quiet; the only people staying were the mercenaries, employed by the Biafrans, some local people and about one hundred staff to look after them. Food and drink was no problem as we had enough in stock to last for six months or more. We did, however, run out of Camembert cheese and the mercenaries threatened the waiter with a gun if he did not produce any. I had to go and calm them down. I must say, mercenaries are a special breed of human being: rough and uncultivated, free-spending and woman-mad. So when some of them did not return after a bombing raid on Lagos, nobody was really sorry at the hotel.

By now we had a team of Red Cross doctors from Switzerland with us, who were of course much more civilised.

To kill time, we remaining six played golf every afternoon. Golf balls were scarce and searching for them when they were lost in the rough sometimes took quite a time. We seldom located them, but were offered to buy them off the caddies the next day. The blighters used to carry the balls under their toes away from the place where we thought they landed and collect them later.

A curfew was imposed from 10.30 p.m. to 6 a.m. every night. We used to meet at different places in the evenings and usually used one car to get back home just before curfew. As roadblocks were also very common in the town itself, and mostly were manned by young girls, we seldom were home at the requested time, which many times resulted in us ending up at a police station until 6 a.m. in the morning. The girls at the roadblocks got used to us and of course we also had a bit of fun with them. First of all we had to leave the car and stand in a line and they asked us to empty our pockets, which we stubbornly refused to do, telling them that if they wanted to see what we carried around with us, they would have to look themselves. This they were quite eager to do, with a lot of giggles from the girls. It became even funnier when one of our number decided to cut out the pockets and see how the girls would react. So of course, we were welcomed with open arms at the roadblocks, which made us break the curfew.

Another time, at a roadblock manned by soldiers, we had a metal print strip printer in the car and they wanted to know what it was used for. So we printed the name of a soldier on the metal tape and stuck it in his helmet. So of course all the others wanted their names on their helmets. After everybody was happy, we drove on, only to be disturbed by a strange noise in the boot of the car. Stopping and opening the boot, we found a machine gun lying there, which one of the soldiers must have placed in his excitement, and forgotten about. We turned the car around and headed straight back to the roadblock.

We could only imagine what would have happened to us at the next roadblock.

The British High Commission transferred to Port Harcourt and was accommodated at the hotel, and as they represented the legal government of Nigeria, were placed under house arrest. I was arrested one morning and charged with being in league with the British because I was seen speaking to the High Commissioner. After some lengthy discussions, I was set free but also placed under house arrest. However, after I complained to the higher authority this was lifted after a short time.

The hotel was near the airport and the Nigerian air force were trying to disrupt the supply of arms so occasionally a DC3 came to bomb the place. We had a heavy machine gun mounted on the roof of the hotel and every time the plane made its appearance, they started shooting, until it was about one and a half kilometres from the target, when they sought safety in the hotel. So the plane took its time and circled the airport once or twice, when the door was opened and the bombs were dropped by hand. The bombing was so inaccurate that it caused very little damage. Most of the bombs exploded in the nearby fields. Having completed its mission the plane headed for home. This was the sign for the machine-gun crew to emerge from their place of safety and start shooting again.

The staff, although business was virtually dead, wanted a salary increase and threatened to strike, but of course this never materialised, as the military threatened to arrest the lot if they proceeded with their threat. The board members called a meeting to discuss the situation and were really frightened when we ordered food and refreshments from the kitchen; they asked me to sample it first in case it was poisoned.

Slowly but surely the Nigerian army closed in on Port Harcourt. They landed some units at the oil terminal at Abor and made their way towards Port Harcourt. I decided the time had come for me to pack my cases and take the chairman at his word about getting me out of the country.

A few days after our discussion, I was told to be ready every night for about a week; they would take me out on an empty plane returning to Luanda from where I could book a scheduled flight to Europe. Having a last look around the hotel, I found a room with wall hangings of real oriental carpets, left behind by its last occupant. I wondered in which mud hut those very costly carpets would end up being used as floor coverings. Some of the guests' safety deposit boxes were still locked. I could see a soldier shooting the lock to gain access to the contents. The food in the cold rooms and stores would be carried off and sold at high prices in the local market. Just as well I wouldn't be there to witness all this. No doubt some of the officers would have a whale of a time getting drunk and making themselves comfortable in the rooms. Some poor innocent staff members would be shot for one reason or another.

So, when I received the signal to proceed to the airport, I left with a heavy heart. There were three emigrants on the plane, a Red Cross doctor, a priest and a nun. An uneventful flight brought us safely to Luanda, where I boarded a flight to Lisbon the same day and a connecting flight to Geneva. What a relief to be back again in peaceful surroundings and away from being watched twenty-four hours a day. A pity that a country with such a great future was torn apart by internal tribalism and power struggles.

Chapter Six

Greece

In the meantime I had been looking around for a new job and was eventually called for an interview to London with a large company, which proved to be successful. I was appointed general manager of a 700-bed holiday village in Greece, which was to open in the spring of 1967. After an introduction course and visits to various company properties, we were off again.

The hotel was not far from Olympia and right on the seashore, with a large sandy beach. It consisted of a main hotel building with about 150 rooms, restaurant, coffee shop, bar and a nightclub. On each side of the main building there were a number of bungalows that could accommodate 400 holidaymakers. The construction was somewhat behind and I did not think that the hotel would open in time. The owners, of course, assured me every day not to worry and they had actually already accepted a number of bookings prior to my arrival, for April.

April arrived and we were a long way away from being able to accept guests. After lengthy and sometimes heated discussions with the owners, who insisted that we could accept the guests, we eventually agreed to accommodate them at another hotel on the island of Crete. As most of the bookings were for large groups arriving at a nearby army airport, which was granted permission to accept civilian flights, I had the thankless task of going and informing the people. I apologised and painted a fantastic picture of the new destination, telling them about the lovely island, the sandy beaches, the food and who knows what else. Anyway, they accepted the facts quite well and without any serious complaints. Back at the hotel, the work made progress but not fast enough, so we were nearly towards the end of May before we could open the hotel for business.

One Greek word I learnt very fast and which was used every

time I checked progress was '*avrio*', which means 'tomorrow'. Another remark I often heard was that the country where you come from, they open a hotel when it is completed, but in Greece we open but are never finished. How true. However, our guests seemed to be happy and enjoyed their holidays. But, as far as management were concerned, we had a number of quite serious problems.

To start with we discovered that the bungalow's electricity installation was not earthed, with the result that guests who had shower facilities received electric shocks every time they took a shower. So we had to supply them with rubber slippers. The swimming pool, which was in great demand, could only be used four or five days a week. The reason for this was that it was filled with seawater pumped directly from the sea. As there was no filtration plant, a film of sun oil and lotion was usually floating on the water after a few days.

Of course, in normal circumstances it is quite easy to drain the pool in the evening, pump water during the night and be in business again the next day. But, of course, not at this hotel. To start with, the pumps were diesel-operated, quite noisy and located near the more expensive bungalows. So pumping during the night was out of the question, because of the racket from the motors. Luckily, we could start about 8 a.m. in the morning, but had to switch the motors off every one and a half hours or so, as they would be running hot. By about 1.30 p.m. we would have to stop pumping because that was when siesta commenced in Greece, and believe me, if you want to avoid having an excited crowd besieging the office because the afternoon siesta is disturbed, you had better stop pumping. Around 6 p.m. you could happily start again until about 9 or 10 p.m. when the tourists who were soaking up the sun all day long were tired and went to bed early. With this problem, it was not surprising that sometimes two to three days went past before the pool is full.

The usual practice to open a new hotel is to have a soft opening to get the staff familiar with the hotel and then have an official opening where you invite VIPs and hope that the staff have had enough training to ensure a smooth opening. We assumed the right time for this would be about the middle of June, and after discussing the programme with the owners, it was decided to invite about 300 guests. They would be accommodated free of charge for two days, invited to a splendid cold buffet lunch and an official dinner with dancing in the evening. Invitation cards were printed and mailed in good time. About two days before the function, I was casually informed that one of the owners had invited an additional one hundred personal guests. Never mind, we will cope, was the reply from other members of the team. The day of the official opening duly arrived. The security guards had strict orders to check all arrivals at the gate to the complex and ask for their official invitation card. Quite a few people had their parents with them, which I was told was an old Greek custom and which we had to accept, like it or not. In the end we ended up with about 500 to look after. Some of the VIPs were high-ranking government officials and ministers, and of course the Archbishop of Athens, who was specially invited to bless the new hotel.

The chef prepared a magnificent and mouth-watering buffet with showpieces and beautiful butter sculptures. It looked a treat.

Word, of course, had gone around about the opening of the hotel and of the VIPs attending the function. So not surprisingly quite a number of peasants came along the beach and across the fields, starting to gather around. About 11.30 p.m. the people assembled by the pool to witness the blessing of the hotel. At the same time, one of the government ministers, who invariably have a number of supporters following them, decided to have a look at the buffet display. The security guards placed in the restaurant to guard the buffet saluted and stood aside. The buffet followed the peasants who followed the minister. We could hardly believe our eyes, seeing people with whole showpieces under their arms and butter sculptures on their heads leaving the hotel. It goes without saying that the whole affair was a complete washout: people waiting for food, people leaving without lunch and checking out in disgust. Although we cleared our fridges of everything we could lay our hands on, there was just not enough food to go around. Luckily the official dinner went off without a hitch and was a great success, but the lunch fiasco could not be reversed.

Labour laws are very strict in Greece. I wonder sometimes why they need the union at all.

The labour inspectors visited the hotel too frequently and it was therefore not surprising that I was summoned to court on a regular basis.

Staff menus were laid down by the labour departments. Over-time over two hours was not permitted without the department being notified in advance. Working rotas for staff required the signature of the inspector and duties couldn't be changed without their permission. Now, at a hotel it is not always possible to work according to the plan, as many factors influence the working day. So you have to alter duties on short notice and to hell with the labour department. This is OK until the blighter arrives without prior notice, checks the duty rota and discovers that Ari is working a morning shift instead of his normal one in the evening. Result: a court summons.

On the day of judgement, I went along with my secretary, who spoke Greek, and after a few words back and forth, I was fined 1,000 drachmas. A visit from the local police informed me that the head porter was a communist and was a bad influence on staff and visitors alike and therefore must be dismissed. Being by that time quite familiar with the labour regulations, which did not allow me to dismiss staff employed for the season without paying them compensation and most likely court proceedings instituted by the staff member, I questioned the police about it.

'Don't worry your head about this, we are fully behind you and support you.'

So it was left to me to find an excuse to dismiss the man with-out revealing the real reason, which made it difficult, as he was a conscientious and hard-working man. Anyway, it had to be done and, as predicted, a court summons arrived on my desk in due course.

'Sorry, sir, you will realise that we cannot support you in this case and, as this is highly political, you have to defend the case without our assistance,' was the reply from the police, when contacted.

To cut a long story short, I was fined 4,000 drachmas com-pensation for wrongful dismissal and 500 drachmas in costs.

Thanking the judge for his consideration in the case, I proceeded to attend to some other business in town. Returning to the hotel about three hours later, I found the chef waiting for me and informing me that a court official had arrived with a lorry, taking away all the meat out of the cold rooms and was now loading the liquor from the stores, 'because you did not settle the fine before leaving court'.

The meat would be dumped in a store, not a cold room, until such time as the fine was paid. I think I've never written a cheque so fast since then. I can just imagine what would have happened if I had not returned in the nick of time: no meat or liquor over the weekend, for over 500 guests. I would have had a riot on my hands.

To the left of the hotel on a hill overgrown with olives and cypress trees stood a byzantine monastery inhabited by six monks. In the morning and afternoon, a large flock of sheep used to graze there, making it a picture of peacefulness and tranquillity.

We soon became friendly with the monks living there, especially with the chief monk.

You entered the monastery through a medieval gate and found yourself in the inner court with the living quarters on the left and the chapel on the right. The courtyard was shaded by Seville orange trees; underneath the largest a table and chairs were arranged, where I usually had my coffee offered by the monks. Although no one spoke English and my knowledge of Greek was very limited, we conversed with the aid of a dictionary.

As I said, we became quite friendly with the monks, so it was not surprising that when matters at the hotel became quite stressful I sought out the tranquillity of the monastery.

One particular afternoon, I recall the head monk standing on the high wall that surrounded the monastery with a pair of binoculars, which apparently he bought off a German tourist the day before, watching the beach.

'What are you looking at?' I shouted at him.

'What do you think I am looking at? The lovely girls in their bathing costumes,' he replied with a big smile on his face. 'You must have seen the notice on the entrance forbidding women entering the monastery while wearing trousers, miniskirts or shorts: I can only see their lovely features through the binoculars!'

I also laughed and accused him of being a dirty old man.

He was particularly fond of my chef's wife and Mavis told me that when the two of them went visiting the monastery he was all over this lady, paying her compliments and being the perfect host. Quite naturally, we discussed matters relating to the hotel as over the weeks he was informed about everything relating to the hotel, even more so since I invited him down and showed him around the premises. Most of my staff went for confession to him and many times I received quite useful hints from him.

'Watch out for chambermaid Angeliki – she stole some sheets from you – the other day one waiter, Vassos, slept with the young tourist girls in their rooms,' were two examples.

Although it rained very seldom in this part of Greece in the summer months, we were surprised by a short but heavy shower one afternoon while enjoying our usual cup of Greek coffee under the musmula tree so we retired to one of the rooms in the monastery. This was the first time I had actually entered the living quarters at all. The room was quite pleasantly furnished with piles of hand-woven tapestries, which were apparently donated to the monastery by the womenfolk from the surrounding villages. As they had no real use for them, they just stored them here.

'Can I have one?' I enquired.

'Go ahead and make your choice,' was the reply.

So when I returned to the hotel a little later I carried under my arm a piece of local handicraft. Before I left, I wanted to know the price. The monk refused any kind of money and after I tried very hard for him to accept some offer, he said, 'All right, I will take your money, but you will never set foot in this monastery again.'

Of course, I did not want to spoil our friendship and thanked him for his generous gift. But I was determined to repay him for his gift, so the next day I climbed the hill again, only this time with a bottle of whisky under my arm, which he accepted with pleasure.

Bernie went to school in Switzerland but spent his summer holidays with us. Shortly after his arrival, I took him to visit the monastery and on the way there we met a local farmer with a young donkey. Bernie seemed to be quite taken with the donkey and, within a few minutes and a short haggling over the price for the animal, Bernie was the proud owner of a donkey.

We named him Avrio and the next day the hotel carpenter built a small stable for him. For a few drachmas I engaged a young boy to tend to the animal, but Bernie was told that he had to take him for a walk every day, because most of the time the donkey was tied to a post with a six-metre-long rope. It should go without saying that Avrio was the main attraction for the tourists when he was taken to the beach. On one occasion I wanted to go to town with the car but was unable to find the car and driver. After waiting and looking around for some time, the driver arrived eventually with Bernie sitting next to him and the donkey tied to the car. When demanding to know what was going on, the simple answer was, 'It is too hot to take Avrio walking, so I asked the driver to take us.'

At the end of the season, Bernie had to return to school in Klosters and we decided to sell Avrio, for whom we found a new owner without great problems. Sometimes when I got up in the morning, I went to the window and shouted, 'Avrio.' In most cases I received a 'hee-haw' from somewhere in the fields. So he had not forgotten us – quite a pleasant feeling.

September had arrived and in a few short weeks the hotel would close again.

I received a letter from the district court asking me to submit a copy of the working permit for my secretary and again the ball was thrown in my court; in other words, I had to get on with it. I reported the facts and was promptly in possession of an order to attend the district court on such and such a day. After deliberating with my secretary, we agreed that she should make a visit to the governor's office and explain to him the situation. Off she went and returned with a smile on her face.

'Don't you worry about it,' she told me. 'The case will be dismissed.'

'How come?' I wanted to know.

'Quite simple,' she explained. 'After I told him the story, he thought about it and after a while confronted me with the question of whether I would be available for a weekend in Athens. I agreed and he promised to exert his powers to squash the matter.'

So at the court hearing we got off with a warning that next time they would not be so lenient. The best part about the whole story is that the secretary left a few days later for England and the governor is still waiting for his weekend in Athens.

Again, other countries, other customs, as in Greece. As already mentioned, the housekeeper was a very attractive and lovely girl. It was not surprising that someone would fall in love with her and in this case it was the assistant manager. He was still married, awaiting a divorce, but this did not stop him from visiting the housekeeper's family and asking for her hand and discussing wedding arrangements. Custom demanded that parents choose a husband for their daughter and he seemed to have been success-ful, confirming that he would be the right man for her, but he did not reveal that he was still a married man, otherwise he would never have been accepted.

Anyway, to cut a long story short, something went sour with his divorce and he was deeply worried. Looking for him one afternoon, he could not be found so we started a thorough search and found him in a pool of blood in one of the bedrooms, luckily still alive but with a high loss of blood. He had tried to kill himself with a shotgun. We rushed him to hospital for emergency treatment, but to my surprise the hospital would give no treat-ment before the payment was made for the blood transfusion. To save him I had no alternative but to pay, but I let them know in no uncertain terms what I thought of their demands.

Another custom, a happier one, is the wedding feast.

Having become part of the local community, we were invited to weddings quite frequently. This meant that I had to make arrangements for some of my managers to take on some of my duties for the weekend. The wedding was taking place on Saturday in the local church and after the ceremony everyone went to the bride's house, where a sumptuous buffet was laid out under the trees, abundant with local food and an enormous amount of drink, usually wine and ouzo. Everyone literally stuffs themselves full with food, accompanied by an equal amount of drink. It did not take long and the party was in full swing. Somebody got the donkeys from the field and rode between the tables and chairs. Another one arrived with a shotgun and a pile of plates, which were thrown in the air and shot at. I did not count how many were hit, but it was fun.

Slowly one or two, including myself, were becoming drowsy. With the booze and the heat, it was not surprising and so we took a nap under some olive trees. By the time we woke up again it was night; electric lights and a large bonfire were burning, a band was playing and people were dancing. The food and drink had been replenished. More and more people appeared from somewhere, refreshed and ready for more fun.

About 4 a.m. things quietened down quite considerably, but no one went home exactly. The womenfolk slept in the house, the men somewhere under the trees and the young ones enjoyed themselves somewhere in a quiet spot. Come morning the whole fun repeated itself again, the same as the previous day, until the early hours of Monday. Don't ask me how much food and drink were consumed – I dare not guess. The only thing I remember is that it took me at least a day or two to recover completely again.

We people from the north of Europe have the habit of saying, 'Come and see us some time' or 'Pass by for a drink', but most of the time this is just a figure of speech and does not mean very much. The contrary exists in Greece, as we found out for ourselves.

When you are invited, they really mean it and quickly become offended if you do not take their invitation seriously. Talking of embarrassing moments recalls certain memories. As I said before, we were quite well known in the nearby village and very often took our meals in the local taverna. We'd enter, the owner would see us and greet us with a loud voice, call us 'Mr and Mrs Miramare', so that everybody would start looking at us and give us a friendly smile. We would then be taken to the best table or he might even ask people to move to other tables for us. He'd place a tablecloth on the table with serviettes, although all the other tables were just bare.

We took our leave at Christmas time and spent a nice time in Lüen. There was plenty of snow that year but it was cold. Bernie joined us over the holidays.

January saw us back in Greece; the bookings for the coming season were coming in and we had a lot of office work to do. Mavis was helping me out with the typing of the correspondence. Opening date was 1 May. Things were a bit easier this year as most of the staff had the experience from the last season.

I had a new secretary of Greek origin with British nationality. The Greek owner assured me I would not have any difficulties if I employed her without applying for a work permit and I took his word for this. The housekeeper, a pretty, young, efficient girl, and the assistant manager were also new. The season passed off without too many problems. Sundays we had our hands full with controlling the locals who flocked to visit the hotel precincts in busloads just to look around. I had to forbid these visits as I received a number of complaints from tourists who were taking a nap in their room during the afternoon, only to be disturbed by some stranger suddenly walking in, having a look around. Strange, I thought, here we are, all the tourists descend on Olympia to see Ancient Greece and here are the Greeks having a look at the largest and most modern holiday complex in the Peloponese.

The season, and with it the summer, came to an end. The hotel closed down, and after a month of cleaning up and taking stock, we settled down for a quiet period. I informed the staff to help me in looking after the premises.

We were still in bed one day when suddenly a plane started circling and spraying the hotel and grounds with a chemical.

'Blimey, they took a long time to start spraying the hotel against mosquitoes,' I said to Mavis, remembering my visit to the provincial governor early in the spring with the request for help to reduce the mosquito problem, which was very bad around the hotel. This was because of the very small dams built by the local farmers to convey water during the dry season, which were a perfect breeding ground for the mosquitoes.

About a week later the rains started, in earnest. Our house was surrounded by water from the flooding of a nearby river and all our rooms on the ground floor of the villa were covered in water. During a check on the bungalows and main building, we found a few leaks where water had entered through the roof but on the whole the damage was not too serious.

We took our meals together with the staff whenever we had the time. The food, which was typically local, was very good and as we both always enjoyed sampling the cuisine of a country, we enjoyed joining them.

Sometimes in the evenings we went looking for octopuses with a three-pronged spear and a large flaming torch. The light shone on the water, attracting the fish, which were then easily speared. One evening the cook suddenly dashed from the kitchen with a roasting pan in his hand, chasing and killing a hedgehog, which he cooked the next day, and this was regarded as a great delicacy by the locals.

As we provided work for about 250 staff, mostly from the local villages, we were looked upon as a kind of benefactor. So when we went out for dinner some evenings, we were sometimes not allowed to pay for the meal, because a member of staff during the past season happened to be at the same taverna and had already generously paid the bill. I must say, I found the Greek people very hospitable, friendly and genuine, sometimes to the point when it became embarrassing. There was the chambermaid who insisted that we join the family for Sunday lunch. We knew they were not exactly rich and they would probably kill their best lamb for the meal, but we dared not refuse, as they would have felt offended.

Majorca

The opening of the Cala Viñas Hotel in Majorca was nearing completion and to assist the management I was asked to help with the preparation for the opening and the initial operation. The fourteen-storey hotel with 250 rooms, large restaurants, a nightclub and a swimming pool overlooked a small inlet with a beach. The sales and marketing department did a very good job and the hotel enjoyed a very good occupancy right from the start.

As with any new property, the Cala Viñas also had teething problems. The lifts broke down quite frequently. The reception and entrance to the hotel was situated in the middle, with the restaurant and entertainment areas, all the bedroom being above these floors. With the lifts out of operation, the guests had to climb at least eight floors to reach their rooms from the swimming pool. Quite a strenuous task, so to make the effort a little easier we would install a bar at the reception and offered sherry and refreshments on the house.

As the hotel was not connected to the main water supply of the nearby town, the water requirements were supplied by bowsers. Although the water was clear and drinkable, some guests preferred to order bottled mineral water with their meals. The manager's table was right next to the restaurant entrance and we made certain always to have a bottle of mineral water on the table to give the impression it would be safer to drink mineral water rather than ordinary water, which also increased sales considerably.

In charge of night duties we had a handsome African. Unknown to us, in the beginning he used to spend considerable time while on duty in the bedrooms of young girls. Of course, we had to terminate his employment and he promptly went to the local labour office to complain. When we were confronted with the complaint and explained that the man spent most of his time in various rooms, the director of the Ministry of Labour wanted to see such a tremendous lover personally. Another thing that stands out in my mind was the new experience of the chairman of the board interrupting the proceedings with the message, 'Gentlemen, the paella is ready and cannot be kept waiting.'

On the whole the hotel went very smoothly, and after a few weeks I left the island for a new assignment.

Chapter Seven

Sri Lanka

After two seasons, the company decided to terminate the contract with the Greek owners and I received orders to report to head office as project manager. I was working together with a team of four other hotel managers and each of us had certain assignments for new hotels. My task was to prepare lists of requirements for large and small equipments for a hotel in Majorca and one in Cyprus. The work was very interesting and of course it had one advantage: I worked normal working hours. We rented an apartment in Edgware and settled down to a daily routine that was the same, day by day. However, although we were living a more settled and organised life, I did miss the hotel business and accepted an offer to proceed to Ceylon (now known as Sri Lanka) as project manager for the country's first international hotel, under construction and to be opened in a few months' time.

Ceylon in those days had some financial problems and any imports were practically stopped. The shops in town had nothing to sell except locally produced goods. The commerce was controlled by the government, which set up large cooperatives and corporations. For the first six weeks, I was on my own as Mavis decided to join me later. I took over the apartment from my predecessor; it was large and situated in a quiet suburb of Colombo. A young Ceylonese was in charge of looking after my well-being and a driver took me around on my business calls.

As I mentioned before, importation of foreign goods was practically nil, but the company somehow obtained permission to bring to the country a new car and to my surprise also a washing machine for the apartment, which at least ensured my clothes were properly washed.

The hotel was situated a few miles from Colombo and the man in charge of the construction fence was a tough German engineer. The whole place was surrounded by a six-foot fence with barbed wire around the top. The entrance was manned twenty-four hours a day by uniformed guards armed with truncheons. Every time I wanted to visit the hotel I was stopped at the gate. Permission was then obtained for me to enter the site. But I was not allowed to wander around freely, and was always accompanied by a guard. The German engineer may have had his reasons for being vigilant as there was a lot of thieving going on. Though I did think treating me like that was going a bit too far. Anyway, there was nothing I could do; he would not change his attitude.

To keep a proper control on his tools, every worker had to sign a receipt for every piece he required to carry out the work, and sign it again once he returned the item. An inventory was taken every evening to ensure nothing was missing.

The hotel being a few kilometres from town, we were not connected to the main water supply and consequently had to find our own source of water. A water diviner was asked to look for water about one kilometre from the hotel, where some small wells were already in use.

So off he went and after about an hour of walking up and down and back and forth, he pointed to a spot where there were indications of abundant water below. A construction firm was employed to sink a well four metres in diameter. After reaching twenty metres, we still did not find any water, so it was decided to dig another ten metres, as surely there must be water. After reaching thirty metres and still not finding a drop of water, work was halted.

It was then decided to buy as many small wells in the vicinity as possible and pour the water into the already constructed large well and from there take the water by pipeline to the hotel. Everything went fine until in the middle of the high season most of the wells dried up. So there we were, back to square one again and we had to start buying water from the city water department and have it delivered by bowsers. To make matters worse, although the water tank at the hotel was big enough to hold enough water to cope with the demand, providing there was a steady flow from the well, we now found some of the bowsers had to wait for quite some considerable time to discharge their load because the tank was full. However, after a while we were able to establish some kind of a system to regulate the delivery of water and make certain there was always enough water in the tank and that the guests were not inconvenienced.

Some months before the opening, we found a motor was missing from one of the cold rooms. The police was called and after some lengthy investigations they had two suspects. Walking past the house where the interrogations took place, I saw the two suspects hanging from a thin rope around their thumbs, suspended about four or five centimetres from the ground. It didn't take long until one of them confessed and the motor was recovered not far from the hotel, buried about a metre under the ground. On talking to the police, their reply was quite simple: 'You in your country have all the modern ways and means to detect criminals. We have nothing like this and to obtain confessions we have to resort to methods which seem barbaric to you.'

I could see their point but still thought it a bit inhumane.

Two of my executives were homosexuals and, as it happened, fancied the same boy. Heated arguments developed between them, each accusing the other of being gay. To prove the opposite, one of them got 'engaged' to a local girl who he used to invite to the swimming pool, much to the amusement of the hotel staff, who found it really funny. The other one of the pair wanted to show that he really did not worry about the boy who caused all the commotion, so went and rented a large beach house where he moved in with about ten young boys. Do not get me wrong, apart from the problems facing us, there were incidents that helped us forget for a while at least.

'Good evening, manager,' a guest greeted me, and praised the good dinner he enjoyed this evening. The only thing that spoiled it to a certain extent, he told me, was that the waiter, when asked to bring mayonnaise for his crayfish, replied with a refusal as the mayonnaise was a main course.

Once Mavis joined me, things got a bit easier as she took over the housekeeping at the apartment. She even made some friends.

We joined the swimming club locally and we sometimes ate lunch together there.

Another nuisance was the thousands of starlings that made their home in and around Colombo. These birds are very greedy and if you did not watch out they would dive at your plate and away would fly your steak or fish. At the swimming pool, it was really bad in this respect. You concentrated more on your food than having a look at some of the nice girls around.

As foreign food was not available, if you were lucky to have friends who returned from a trip abroad with a tin of instant coffee, you had to keep quiet about it, otherwise you had a lot of unexpected guests dropping in for a cup of coffee.

Things were that bad that when Mavis received a tin of Heinz baked beans as a Christmas present from a friend, she was quite thrilled about it.

If you were invited for a dinner and the host had a bottle of wine available, you usually had a small glass each (sherry) for a starter and tea with the meal.

Being manager of the first international hotel in the country, I was able to obtain an import license for foreign food and liquor for 10,000 pounds sterling.

I placed my order in Singapore, and as the goods arrived at the port, we went down to see the offloading. I heard some quite disgusting stories and reports about the offloading system of the local dockers.

True enough, as the first load was lowered by the crane, the box suddenly dropped from a height of about three feet to the ground, breaking open the wooden box and spilling the contents to the ground. Before you could say 'pop', the goods had disappeared. I did not mind so much about the amount of money lost, as the goods were insured, but I was annoyed by the loss of the food and drink.

Word got quickly round the town that the hotel received food and drink that had not been available for years. Consequently our bar was occupied more by the locals than tourists. The first alcohol to run out was rum and we had to reserve about one or two bottles for only foreign guests.

My brief was to employ the required local staff three months before the opening and ensure that they had sufficient training and knowledge of their duties before the hotel received its first guests.

On our order for equipment was a number of chambermaid trolleys and, before painting and finishing our bedroom corridors, we had to teach our staff to push the trolleys along without touching or damaging the walls. Instead they liked riding the trolleys. When asked to clean a bathtub, they stepped right in to clean the bath.

To provide our staff with lunch, we contracted a local eating place to send packed lunches to the hotel, until such time as our kitchens were operational. One day, a sample was brought to my office and it was really disgusting. To start with, the food was packed in newspaper, already soaked from the greasy food, and when I opened it, the food was crawling with maggots. Despite our daily problems, everything went along quite satisfactorily and we were able to welcome our first guests on schedule.

However, the teething problems were only beginning. The electricity supply fluctuated according to the demand of the whole area. Frequent upsurging was quite common, with the result that seventy per cent of our cold-room motors were burnt out in the first three months.

As these motors were of the latest type available on the European market, they could not be repaired locally. Replacements took at least six months to arrive as you first of all required an import license and secondly, which was more difficult to obtain, the necessary foreign exchange. We were able to arrange storage facilities with a local firm to store our meat and other perishables, but had to travel five miles every day to fetch our requirements. We had a stand-by generator, but this unit ceased to work after about three months in operation. The cause: salt in the contacts caused by seawater, as the unit was stored on the deck of the ship when shipped to Ceylon and not properly protected.

Not only was the upsurge in the electricity one problem, the more annoying problem was the power cuts. Without any electricity, no air conditioning, no water distribution and dealing with all the complaints, it was very trying to keep a cool and collected head. To flush the toilets, seawater had to be collected in buckets from the beach about one hundred yards away. Water for cooking was fetched from the water tank.

When the power cuts happened in the morning, we had to take hot water to every room for washing.

To offer some entertainment, it was decided to hold a dinner dance every Saturday evening. We engaged a band and had quite a good turnout. I entered the restaurant about 10 p.m. to find it nearly empty. I wanted to know the cause of this and was told the band was so lousy that all the guests after dinner had left. So we insisted as a condition that any band we engaged in future had to pass an audition before being accepted.

On Sundays we had a buffet, at which the chef used some imported fruit for the decoration of cakes and so on. The locals just picked off the fruit and left the cake. We could sell two half peaches as a sweet for up to fifty shillings or Danish caviar for seven pounds (sterling) per two-and-a-half-ounce tin, so large was the demand.

One of the annual highlights in Ceylon is the Perahara in Kandy in the highlands of the country. This is a Buddhist festival that lasts for about ten days, with a daily procession of dancers and drummers in colourful costumes and about thirty or forty elephants similarly dressed. The elephant belonging to the temple carries on his back a tooth of Buddha encased in a cage made of pure gold. Being a carrier of such a highly prized holy treasure, he is never allowed to step on bare ground. Temple attendants use two pieces of cloth, about a twenty-foot long and five feet wide, which are placed on the ground before the holy elephant, and as soon as he has stepped on the second, the first is removed and brought to the front again. In this way he always walk on the carpets.

The last procession takes place at night, which is quite impressive, as is the one held in the daytime with all the elephants decorated with strings of small electric lights and the various groups illuminated by torchbearers. Needless to say that the town is packed with thousands of people.

I was lucky to have some good connections and was therefore able to get a room for the night in a local hotel. My driver had to sleep in the car.

I took the chance to be taken around the hotel and was astonished to note the primitive equipment the staff had to cope with. The stove in the kitchen was heated by wood and the whole area was black from smoke. Old wooden tables were used for the preparation of food. The floor was uneven and of concrete, with a wooden plank in front of the stove. The staff wore dirty uniforms and tennis shoes or none at all. A good breeding place for millions of bacteria. Maybe because the menu consisted mainly of curry dishes, they did not have any cases of food poisoning, or perhaps the people who ate there were hardened against the conditions.

As always during our travels and transfers, we did need excess baggage allowance, which did come quite high sometimes. Remembering the trials at the airport from my earlier days in Ceylon, we were anxious to know if they still existed. We did not have to worry this time, however, for as soon as we arrived at the airport, we were approached by the 'little man', we handed over our tickets and all luggage and proceeded to passport control. The little man was already waiting for us in the departure lounge with the tickets and receipt. A ten-dollar note handed over concluded the business and he was gone to find another customer. I remarked to Mavis that it just showed old customs take a long time to change, although there are stiff penalties for anyone being caught.

Chapter Eight

Jamaica

In the meantime, the Forte and Trust House companies merged and some internal changes were taking place just as my assignment came to an end in Ceylon. Back in London, we were accommodated in a company hotel. I was offered a position in the newly created Planning and Project Department or a job as general manager in Jamaica. Three weeks' introductory work at the project department confirmed that I really preferred hotel management. Although the job at the project department did offer regular hours of work five days a week with every weekend off, the busy hotel life, with all of its challenges, I preferred. A short visit to the hotel site in Jamaica made me decide definitely to remain in my chosen profession.

A short time later, Mavis and I arrived on the beautiful island in the Caribbean. On the way to Jamaica, we had a familiarisation trip over Nassau, Miami and Bermuda, and we enjoyed staying and seeing the hotels on these islands. We found a terraced house with a swimming pool without much difficulty and settled in with not too much hassle.

The Jamaica Pegasus, as the hotel was to be called, was situated in New Kingston within a very short distance of the Sheraton and Skyline hotels. It offered accommodation for 600 persons with other facilities such as a coffee shop, restaurant, nightclub, swimming pool, a pub and a shopping arcade with extensive conference and banqueting facilities, too.

Everything proceeded accordingly and we were scheduled to open in about twelve months' time.

My first priority was to interview and engage my management team. Appointments were finalised and I travelled to London for selection interviews. The ones selected joined me about six months later in Jamaica.

To start, I rented an office in the building of the Jamaica Hotel

Association, engaged a secretary, who was performing satisfactorily. One day, sitting in my office, a smart-looking girl appeared and without much ado asked me plainly, 'Do you need a secretary?' She had a professional approach and appearance that appealed to me right away and within a week she was taking over as executive secretary. I must say, I never regretted my decision, because she was a real asset to my office. There was not much dictating from me, as she seemed to know how to deal with most correspondence. Just a small note saying 'stuff him' from me if a letter arrived that I did not approve of resulted in a two-page letter, implying diplomatically that the correspondent should 'get stuffed'.

As with so many unforeseen problems, the construction company experienced some difficulties in completing the hotel as planned and the opening was delayed for a further three months.

By chance, the manager at the Guyana Pegasus left the company and as I was somewhat at a loose end for three months, we again packed our suitcases to transfer to Georgetown in Guyana.

Guyana Pegasus, Georgetown

The hotel, a joint venture between BOAC (British Overseas Airways Corporation) and Trust House Forte situated in Guyana's main city, Georgetown, was the only modern hotel in the country. Built right at the waterfront, the hotel was actually below sea level; it was strange to relax at the swimming pool and see a large ship passing above you towards the harbour. The amenities of the hotel were limited, with well-appointed bedrooms, a small lounge, restaurant, pool bar, terrace, banqueting rooms and a shop, mainly visited by business people. Local airlines operated inland flights to one or two remote places within the country.

We had the opportunity to fly to the savannah together with the local BOAC manager. The Dakota providing the service was halfway full with commercial guests: livestock on the right side of the plane with passenger seats on the left. The so-called airport was a small runway without buildings. A joker had provided a seat with a small covering of a roof and made it the departure lounge. The guest house was comfortable. The kitchen, built from local material, stood slightly apart from the main house. An open hole in the wall was the window and all around the house were chickens, geese, cats and dogs looking for food. Anything the cook did not need, he threw out of the window and all were fighting, eagerly awaiting. We learned quite a lot about life in the savannah from the owner of the guest house.

As the savannah can only support a limited population, the tribe controls the birth of male and female children. If it is agreed that only male babies are allowed to live, the mother has to kill the baby if it is a girl. Before the birth of a baby is expected, the mother is locked in and accommodated in a special hut and remains there until the birth of the child. Food is provided through a hole in the wall.

Elderly men, if they are a burden, will be put in a small boat and sent over the very high Kaieteur Falls nearby. Cruel, but the only way to control the population.

During one of our evening strolls through the countryside, we were passed by a local Amerindian who greeted us with a cheerful 'Good evening' in English. Surprised, we stopped and discovered that he spoke very good English. During the conversation, he revealed that his name was McKenzie and that his father was a Scotsman who had married a local girl.

The American Culture Centre held a weekly cocktail party where the American mission entertained the local girls. Young girls tried to angle an American to marry them and obtain a resident's permit to settle in America. In most cases, it was agreed that, once the girl had been in the States for a certain time, divorce proceedings were started.

Another way to leave the country was to organise a party at the hotel, charging an entrance fee and with the proceeds obtained it was hoped to have sufficient funds.

A golf course was available just outside the town. The course was heavily waterlogged and had a number of small ponds, sometimes inhabited by snakes. The rule allowed golfers to engage two caddies: one of them to retrieve any ball that landed in one of the ponds and the other to carry on with the player. Golf balls were rather rare to obtain and also rather expensive so we were not happy to lose balls.

Jamaica – Return

On my return to Jamaica, the selected management team started arriving and we settled down to prepare our future policy, how to run the hotel and attend to all pre-opening requirements.

Local staff were selected and required three months before the opening to report for work and training.

Going through the employment forms, to make final decisions and see if the person had the right qualifications for the position, I had to laugh as under the heading 'sex', one applicant had written 'three or four times a week'.

The great day of the official opening was upon us before we realised.

About 400 persons were invited, and two young girls were chosen to present flowers to the main speech givers. Just before presenting the large bouquet to the Prime Minister, one little girl called to her mother, 'I want to make pee pee.'

Of course, we wanted to make a big impression on the public and, knowing the easy way of life in the Caribbean, we chose waitresses for the pub with fuller figures and large breasts with a deep cut in the blouse, so that when she bent over one had a good view of her bosom. We had, to our surprise, a little resistance from the locals but they soon got used to the idea.

The nightclub took off like a bomb and as a special attraction we proposed to engage a topless band from Miami. Everything was all right until I went to the Minister for Tourism for a work permit. 'Fantastic,' was his reply but unfortunately a bit too much provocation for the nightclub.

The Sheraton Hotel had a serious problem with prostitution. Girls used to sit by the entrance to the hotel in the evening, offering their services to guests and even knocked on doors during the course of the night. The tip-off of single rooms occupied by males was given them by reception for a small fee.

The Minister for Tourism, who became a regular patron of the hotel, asked me to keep out these undesirable persons.

A certain guest, of course, wanted to know why they were not allowed to take bed partners to the rooms and was quite annoyed when told the reasons. So something had to be done and we looked around for some good-looking and very presentable young ladies who were glad to earn a few dollars a night as hostesses. The idea was that they would entertain the guest at the nightclub with a commission on the total amount of the guest's bill. If they wanted to hop into bed with him, that was their own affair. We kept an album of the girl's photographs at the night manager's office and if necessary the guest could make his choice.

The girl was then telephoned and usually arrived within minutes. Because the girls were quite refined, no one could object to their presence in the club, as they knew how to behave.

I was told by other hotel managers that Jamaicans are not reliable and not committed to their jobs. At the Pegasus, we strived to make our labour force highly motivated and productive. To achieve this, a number of new ideas were developed. One was to form a canteen committee to design menus that suited the local staff and that taught them to work within the budgeted figure. A staff benevolent fund was created. Every member paid monthly one dollar into this fund. Requests for urgently needed assistance were again channelled to a special committee to arrive at a decision if the request was to be granted, the repayment period, or if the money was to be paid out without repayment for those with very little or limited finances.

Arrangements were concluded with manufacturers of clothes and shoes where staff could purchase items at cost prices plus ten per cent. Regular meetings were held with all staff to air certain problems. Every manager, including me, had to take turns on a weekly basis to eat in the staff canteen. All of these measures achieved the required results and we had a happy and contented workforce.

The labour union movement was very strong on the island and they tried very hard to organise our staff to join them, but without success initially. This was until the union members started to beat up some staff members when they left work and, in one case or two, burn down their houses.

So in the end I advised staff to join the union and we concluded a contract with the officials to deduct the monthly fee from salaries direct. Needless to say, I had a visit from the leader nearly every week but never any from the appointed stewards.

During one meeting, the union leader informed me he was off to London, but did not know where to stay.

'Come back in a week and I will have something for you,' I said.

A number of telexes went off to various hotels in the UK asking for free accommodation for a family of four. All were very cooperative and on his return we had a complete programme ready for him. After the trip, he came back full of enthusiasm and recounted the lovely time he had had. However, this did not make him realise that by accepting my offer he had played right into my hands; afterwards every time we had a problem which was a little complicated, I referred to the holiday in the UK and everything was usually dropped as not important.

Mavis and I had ample time to see the island and I took extra days off due to me during the time Bernie spent his holidays with us. Providing any hotel had free rooms, a phone call to the manager secured complimentary accommodation throughout the island. This arrangement applied to every member hotel of the Hotel Association. The golf clubs were never left behind as there were some really first-class courses all over the island and we spent many hours trying to hit the ball.

The security problem, however, was one of the most serious I had ever experienced so far.

Everywhere you went armed guards were guarding the premises, even at hotels. I refused to have armed guards around the hotel, refused even a bulletproof cashiers' shield. What was the point if a gunman got hold of a guest and threatened to shoot if the money was not forthcoming to play the hero and have a dead client? So my instructions were to hand over the money and press the alarm button that activated the nearby police station. Although it never happened to us, restaurants were frequently raided by gangs. Three or four men would burst in with loaded shotguns, demanding that every guest lay flat on the floor. Systematically, every person was robbed of their wallet, jewellery and any other worthy items.

At night I drove with locked and closed windows and when the way was clear never stopped at a red traffic light, otherwise a shotgun was suddenly pointing at you, demanding your money.

Matters got even worse and started losing the island very-much-needed revenue from tourism, when the gangs started to attack tourist buses on the famous west coast, which was extensively reported by the American media. The government tried every means, within the law, to master the situation but without much success. Unemployment and low salaries drove the youngsters to take the law into their own hands.

Shops were set alight and looted, and when the fire brigade arrived the fire hoses were cut. Consequently the police became very trigger-happy and in one incident killed seven innocent people travelling in a car with the exhaust backfiring, mistakenly thinking that a gang was shooting at them. To safeguard the weekly payments for our staff, we had a contract drawn up whereby the security company received the pay cheque from us, collected the required cash from the bank, put the money in pay packets and paid it out to the staff at the timekeeper's office, with two armed guards with machine pistols either side of the pay counter.

There was a favourite trick by some guests to obtain money from hotels by false means.

We had one such case when a young lady threatened to sue the hotel because she was raped there.

When the case was reported, the chief security officer was sent to investigate.

He found the room in disorder, the telephone cord ripped from the wall and a very distressed lady sitting on the bed. In the meantime, I called the hotel doctor, and when he finished his examination, he reported that the rape was fabricated and that nothing wrong had happened.

As a precaution against such happenings we established a system by which each hotel informed the others of the person's identity, passport number and other important factors. Like most governments in developing countries, they wanted to see local people taking over important positions from foreign expatriates. Jamaica was no exception and each manager except the general manager had a local person as understudy. During my term of duty in the Pegasus, I saw very competent local persons taking charge of food and beverages and the sales department, and both were women.

As mentioned previously, we were very strict to keep out the prostitutes lingering around the hotel. A customer caught with a girl in his room was asked in the morning to pay his bill and leave the hotel. On one such occasion, I get involved because the deputy manager was on holiday. Up to the room I went and informed the guest of the hotel rules and asked him to settle his bill.

During the course of the morning I received a call from the Ministry of Tourism that the minister wished to see me. He asked me if I made a guest leave the hotel. I acknowledged this and was then asked if I knew who the person was. I did not know the guest's name. I was then told he was Prime Minister of a Caribbean island. I apologised for the way I handled the situation and offered to receive the person again at the hotel, only to be told he had already left Jamaica.

I think to a certain extent I was lucky to get away so lightly.

Chapter Nine

Cyprus

Our next port of call was Cyprus. The company had just completed a holiday village called the Golden Sands in Famagusta on the island of Cyprus. I was asked if I would be interested in taking over as general manager, as the one who was originally appointed and acted as the 'opening manager' – that is, got everything ready to have an operational unit ready for opening day – had been transferred to the States. As I already had connections from some years earlier, as project manager, to this hotel, it did not take much to persuade me to accept the position. To keep it short, the hotel had 900 beds in the hotel complex and bungalows, an entertainment centre for residents and non-residents, four restaurants, two coffee shops, three bars, a nightclub, a self-service restaurant, two beach bars, two swimming pools, four tennis courts, minigolf, its own motorboats, pedaloes and waterskiing facilities, and also a piazza for local entertainment.

We, that is, Mavis and I, arrived just a few days before the official opening, at which Archbishop Makarios, the President of the Republic, would be present.

Now there was a lot to be done and the workers were present twenty-four hours a day at the site to have everything ready for the big day. Police officials were everywhere to organise the safety and security of the President.

The actual day of the ceremony passed peacefully and without incident for the 500 guests invited and by the next morning we were ready to welcome our first guests. We had an apartment in town, as no manager's suite was available at the hotel, but I had already made it known to the company that I would prefer to live at the premises.

Unknown to me, the owner of the house where our top-floor flat was situated was not much in favour with the Greek-orientated EOKA organisation under General Grivas. So it came to us as a great shock when one night we were awakened by an explosion in front of the house. The shops on the ground floor were totally destroyed, but luckily we escaped unhurt, although one or two windows at the flat were broken. As the lease of the flat was about to expire, we started looking around and found a lovely penthouse flat with a large terrace, ideal for cocktail parties and other gatherings.

In the meantime, the hotel was about two thirds occupied and I must say everything went smoothly. In a holiday hotel, the guests are more relaxed than in comparison with a business hotel, where everything has to be geared to perfection. As we were still in early spring, most guests preferred to sit and lounge around the swimming pools, instead of lazing on the beach; at the pool they were protected from the cool winds that come off the sea.

Although we had about 300 sun loungers, we found it was not enough to go round. The German tourists developed a system to ensure that they got most of the chairs before all the others. It worked quite simply: one got up early in the morning and rented about ten chairs, arranged them around the pool and sat there watching over them while his other friends enjoyed their breakfasts. Once they arrived at the pool, he then went for his meal. Naturally this aggravated other guests and I received many complaints about it. The only advice I could give them was to introduce the same system themselves. Another suggestion they had was that we should only issue one chair per person, collected himself from the store. Every week we had a tennis tournament with a small silver cup as prize for the winner. If a German and an Englishman were playing in the final, you could feel the loaded atmosphere and the rivalry between these two nations.

The chef decided as a way of an attraction to load a small local carriage with fruit and vegetables just in front of the grill room, which was situated in the entertainment centre. However, this didn't last for long as most of the fruit and vegetables were stolen by people staying at holiday flats; they probably found it a good way of helping to stretch their holiday budget.

Bernie was due soon to join us, as the summer school holidays were about to begin. In the meantime, the political trouble had increased, bombing and disturbances were getting worse and there was talk about a Turkish invasion.

What was a rumour was soon confirmed in a few days by the landing of Turkish troops at Kyrenia. The Cyprus army was not equipped to halt the advances of this superior force and soon Turkish troops surrounded Nicosia.

We had about 500 guests at the hotel and we had strict orders not to let them wander around outside. Most of the staff left to join the army and I was left with about twenty staff to look after 500 guests. Emergency procedures were introduced, and guests were required to make their own beds and collect their food direct from the kitchen. We arranged all kinds of indoor enter-tainment for them to pass the time.

The United Nations force started evacuating stranded tourists, starting at hotels near the port, which had already seen attacks from the Turkish air force. Our hotel had experienced machine-gun fire.

Blackout was ordered by the police but some of the residents of the hotel didn't care much about it and left their lights showing from the windows. A telephone call from the police headquarters warned us that should any light be seen, after ten minutes, the army had orders to shoot at them. So the only thing left was to cut off the electricity by switching off the mains switch.

Candles were distributed with strict orders not to have them burning when, due to excessive heat in the rooms, the windows were opened.

It was now three days that the guests had been virtually pris-oners of the hotel and I decided to contact the British commanding officer, well known to me, of Camp Mile Two for assistance. He promised to do everything possible to evacuate the guests the next day. As promised, the first army trucks arrived about midday and by evening all had left. Bernie, who had just arrived one week before the invasion, left with Mavis and so did most of my remaining staff.

That evening, three Cypriots and myself were the only people occupying the hotel. The only incident I recall was when an angry guest came to my office about 6 p.m. one evening during the emergency, complaining about the service and general conditions at the hotel and demanded to be moved to another hotel.

I tried to explain to him that the Golden Sands was the only hotel still operating but without effect. As he became more and more angry, I called the local police commander, who promised to come along himself to talk some sense to the complainer. He listened to the guest's remarks and replied, 'If you want to leave the hotel with your luggage and find another hotel by yourself, you are welcome to do so. But remember the curfew is about five minutes away and if you are on the street, you are likely to be shot. What is it now? Are you going or are you staying? Keep your mouth shut and appreciate what the hotel is doing to make you people as comfortable as possible until you are evacuated.'

So what else could the complainant do but wait like all the other guests?

Two days after all the guests had left, a ceasefire was arranged and some of the staff reported back for duty. We started a thorough clean-up, and piled up the luggage that was left behind, as only one piece of luggage per person was allowed on the plane, into three rooms on the third floor.

However, the ceasefire was of short duration and over the radio we heard that the Turkish troops were advancing on Famagusta, causing panic within the local population, who fled the town to safer places inland and to the British military bases on the island.

A phone call from the British Camp Two Commander informed me late afternoon that Turkish tanks had been reported entering the Turkish sector of Famagusta and if I promised to leave within the next hour with my remaining three staff to the safety of the British base, he would send an armoured car to get us out.

Hurriedly we packed some food and blankets in my car and the hotel van and left the hotel. We were forced to spend the first night in a forest just outside Dekalia, the British base, as entry was stopped until early morning.

Next morning we entered the base, but informed the military police that we would not like to stay at the refugee camp; instead we would prefer to stay within the borders of the base as we had everything required to be comfortable.

So we settled down under some shady trees and awaited new

developments. I was worried about the food stored at the hotel and the papers I had left behind, and contacted my military friend at the base, with the unusual request that he obtain permission from the local Turkish commander for me to enter the town and the hotel.

The day after, we decided to try to enter the town on our own through fields and along the beach. We reached a point about three quarters of a mile from the hotel when a grenade from a tank was shot in our direction, which made us abandon our attempt rather hurriedly.

Permission to enter the hotel was granted sooner than expected. I was instructed to report to the nearest Turkish checkpoint on the main road to Famagusta. There I was told to proceed very slowly to the hotel, not exceeding five to ten kilometres per hour. Apparently, Greek Cypriots were entering the town to loot and the army had orders to shoot anything at all suspicious. The trucks were already in front of the hotel as I arrived; before entering the premises, the British soldiers made a thorough search of the hotel. The food was then transferred to the trucks. The Turks were mostly interested in dry and tinned goods, which left the goodies such as meat, fish and refrigerated items to the British. All this must have been a welcome change for the chef to vary his menus for the next few days. Strangely enough nobody was interested in the liquor stores, so all the contents were left behind.

Everyone was still hoping to return to Famagusta very shortly and new rumours were circulating in the camp every day. We idled the days away by eating, sleeping and swimming in the large water tank next to our camp. Fresh meat was no problem – especially lamb, as one of my staff was quite an expert at slipping out at night and killing one of the lambs that were grazing around the fields. He even made money by selling melons from a field adjoining our camping site to the refugees living at the proper camp. When some of them just wanted to help themselves to the fruit, it did not stop this fellow from making a complaint to the camp commander, asking him to tell his guards to stop people from stealing his melons.

The chances of returning to Famagusta within the near future became more remote every day, so we decided to leave the island for England. The situation by now had returned somewhat to normal and more and more refugees were leaving the camp as the government offered alternative accommodation on the island. Some moved in with friends and relations.

We discovered that a ship was leaving every four days from Limassol to Athens in Greece and we made arrangements to purchase four tickets, which proved more difficult than expected, as many people were leaving the island by the only way open to them as all airports were closed.

My head hall porter, one of my party, was given the task of using his knowledge and influence to secure tickets as quickly as possible. So off he went and returned with the news that he was able to purchase a private cabin for myself with room for the car on the next trip. For the rest, the only way he was able to secure the trip was to sign them up as crewmembers, working as waiters on the journey, which suited them all right.

The day before departure, we shut down our camp, gave away what was left and drove to Limassol. We had a good meal at a taverna and started looking for accommodation for the night. Again, our successful head porter was sent off. As we had roughed it for about four weeks, I thought we deserved something good and asked him to find rooms with air conditioning. While we waited for him to return, we finished off our meal with plenty of wine and local brandy. Again, our messenger returned with the good news that everything was arranged, and after drinking and enjoying ourselves for the rest of the afternoon we transferred to the hotel in the evening.

I myself hit the hay quite early in the evening, as the excess wine and liquor consumed during the afternoon took its effect.

Blow me, I couldn't sleep very much during the night because nearly every hour there was a knock on my door by a pretty girl wanting to know if I wanted some company. When telling my crew of my experience during breakfast, I was informed that this hotel was the town's brothel.

We boarded ship later in the day. We were due to sail in the early evening. Instead of the normal 300 passengers the ship was allowed to carry, there must have been double that figure on-board. People

The Mount Elgon Hotel, Mbale, Uganda.

The Apolo Hotel, Kampala, Uganda.

The Presidential Hotel, Enugu, Nigeria.

The Presidential Hotel, Port Harcourt, Nigeria.

The Cala Viñas Hotel, Majorca, Spain.

The Miramare Olympia Beach Hotel, Pirgos, Greece.

The Pegasus Reef Hotel, Colombo, Sri Lanka.

The Jamaica Pegasus Hotel, Kingston, Jamaica.

The Golden Sands Hotel, Famagusta, Cyprus.

The Riyadh Palace Hotel, Riyadh, Saudi Arabia.

The President Hotel, Johannesburg, South Africa.

The Grand Hotel, Manchester, United Kingdom.

The Agador Hotel, Agadir, Morocco.

The Hotel Basma, Aswan, Egypt.

The Lake Victoria Hotel, Entebbe, Uganda.

were sleeping everywhere, in the lounges on the open decks – in other words wherever there was just enough space to lie down. I felt somewhat embarrassed to have a cabin all to myself. There were five sittings for every meal and my crew must have had plenty of work, as the dining room seemed never to close. When they brought me such items as fresh fruit and other delicious items that were not on the menu, I had to order them to abstain, because some of the other passengers noticed what was happening and although I did not understand what they said, I could quite imagine what they discussed.

The trip to Greece passed without incident. We made a brief stop at Rhodes, where some of the passengers disembarked, and arrived in Piraeus the next day. Here I bade farewell to my staff, who made their way to London by rail. For myself, I drove to Patras and bought a ticket to Italy on the ferry leaving that same evening. Luckily enough, I had my credit cards with me or I would have been stranded, because I had no cash on me. Once in Italy, I hit the autostrada and proceeded home. As there existed no speed limit on these roads, I was able to speed along at 160–180 kilometres per hour. I had never driven the Rover that fast and I was very surprised at the road holding of the car. I made it home the same day, towards evening. I felt good, although it took me a few days to shake off the experiences of the previous few weeks.

Head office wanted to see me as soon as possible, so after a few days' rest I took to the road.

I received quite a hero's welcome from my bosses and after making my report I was told to take leave and await further instructions in due course.

After about four weeks' enjoyable leave, I reported back to head office. It was decided I should return to Cyprus as things had quietened down and take charge of the office my personnel manager had opened in Nicosia. This was to deal with out-standing matters such as wages due, settlements of bills and most importantly to try to gain access to the hotel in Famagusta.

The last request proved more difficult than expected. For about three weeks, nearly every day, I crossed the only checkpoint at the green line and visited one office after another to obtain permission to proceed to Famagusta. In the end, the Turks must have been very browned off with my daily pestering and issued me with the necessary papers and a guide to take care of me.

On our way to Famagusta, we must have been stopped a dozen times by the military. On arrival in the town, which gave the impression of being ghost town, we had to report to the local commander. His office was in the main square of the Turkish-occupied section of the town and the surrounding houses were used by the troops as sleeping quarters. The square itself was used as a parade and training place. I waited in the car while my guide went to see the commanding officer and I had plenty of time to watch the young recruits being taught military discipline.

At the time, they were being taught to march to the command, 'Left, right, left, right.' On closer inspection, I noticed the leading man of the platoon had a clove of garlic fastened on his left trouser leg and an onion on the other. I tried to find an explanation to this and was later, on the return of my guide, told the reason. Apparently the young soldiers being trained were coming from remote areas of Turkey and also quite illiterate. As they were unable to understand the command 'Left, right, left, right', the training officer shouted 'garlic, onion', until such time as they were able to march properly. Discipline seemed to be quite strict, because I never saw any soldier walking when given a command, but they were almost running every time.

I was also told the Turkish soldier was one of the best in the world. Firstly, most of them had only limited education and during their training they were taught rigidly to obey orders to the last, and when asked to fight would obey without asking questions. Accompanying us to the hotel was a Turkish soldier with a fully loaded rifle and his orders were to open any door first before letting us enter. Nothing seemed to be disturbed and I found nearly every thing just as I left it. The Union Jack that we had hoisted on the rooftop and the sign at the door saying 'British Property' had been removed. On closer inspection, many office doors had been broken down as we had locked them all on departure. Somebody had tried to open the main safe, but without success and in frustration had written across the door 'fuck you'.

As we still had some time to spare after our tour around the hotel, we decided to visit Kyrenia. What a change from the last time Mavis and I spent some very pleasant hours in this nice beauty spot. With luck we found a café open, but otherwise everything was closed.

Together with my personnel manager Andy, in Nicosia we had enough work to cope with: the various requests for outstanding salaries, checking bills and so on.

The local population was still very much on edge and the slightest rumour about the Turkish army movement made them flee town. The hope that everything would be back to normal in the not-too-distant future was in everybody's mind. The local press was always full of such hopes and I used to call the people's expectations of an early settlement 'torture of hope'.

It must have been about two months since my last visit to Famagusta when London asked me to make a further visit to the hotel. To my great surprise, the Turkish authority welcomed my request, and asked me to take up residence in the Turkish sector of Famagusta, open an office at the hotel and engage one or two staff to help me.

Of course, this was out of the question as the hotel belonged to the Cypriot government and they would never have agreed that I work for the Turks. What lay behind the offer I could only guess. Maybe the Turks wanted to open up the Greek section of Famagusta for tourists entering from Turkey, as they had done so with most hotel in occupied areas.

Anyway, I stayed about four days in Famagusta, visiting the hotel every day and sleeping at night at the Salamis Bay Hotel. I usually went to eat at a taverna in the fort of Famagusta and must say found some quite delightful small tavernas within the small narrow streets, with good and appetising local food and wine. It was my intension to collect all the luggage left behind in the hotel by the tourists during the invasion and return it to the owners. But some looters had entered the hotel, presumably during the night with the local policeman looking the other way (or perhaps they took part in the looting), had opened the luggage, taken away the most valuable items and strewn the rest all over the place.

Windows had been broken to gain access, and in the kitchen pigeons had made themselves at home.

All the valuable leather clothes were taken and I was certain I had seen Turks walking in the street wearing them. On the streets of the town, especially the beachfront, bushes were growing on the sand, which was blown by the wind from the beach.

Curtains were fluttering from broken windows of the building and the whole town had already started to decay. I wonder what it looks like now, thirty-six years after the invasion. There was not much more I could do and so I returned again to Nicosia and shortly afterwards to London to await a new assignment.

Chapter Ten

South Africa

My going to Johannesburg to take over the President Hotel was prompted by the transfer of the man in charge back to the U.K.

My briefing was quite a bucketful. The hotel was losing money and somehow it had to be turned around. That in short words was my task, and as I say quite a bucketful.

To enable me to get to know the hotel in the eyes of a visitor, it was suggested that I should go to Johannesburg ten days before taking over. My brief was to visit the hotel daily, eat there and sit in the lobby to get the feeling of the hotel, talk to guests and at the same time, note problem spots – but not to give any indication of my future role to anyone at the hotel. At the same time, I was to stay at competition hotels.

My first impression was very favourable. The furnishings and decor were really luxurious. However, on closer inspection, you were able to notice that everything was a little neglected and a coat of paint here and there would not do any harm. What impressed me was the Transvaal Room Restaurant. A real beauty in decor and furnishings and, as I was told by local people and hotel managers, the best restaurant in town, if not the best in the whole of South Africa. The manager, a most capable man, whom I learnt later to respect very highly, was of Italian origin and he had the flair, personality and pleasantness you find in persons from this part of Europe. Without hesitation, I have not in my many years come across a better maitre d'hôtel. His capabilities were reflected in the repeated praise from regular clients. This flair was especially appreciated by the ladies. He just knew how to make them welcome; in other words, to make a little fuss of them: kissing their hands on arrival, mentioning how good they looked and presenting them with a red rose upon departure. He could describe a dish in such detail the mouth started to water before you even touched the food. The chef's recommended dish of the day he sold like hot cakes, at his recommendation.

He knew just what to do in a difficult situation. I recall one incident with a party occupying a corner table. A lady of the party called him across.

'My good man, I have just seen a mouse showing itself in the corner.'

So what does he do? He goes over to the corner.

'Nelly,' he said, 'you know your dinner time is after 11 p.m. so please don't come and upset my client and keep to your appointed time.'

Smiles all around and the matter was forgotten.

He was rather surprised when, having looked after me for about ten days, on the day of my taking over, the outgoing manager introduced me as his successor. The hotel was built about ten years previously as a luxurious five-star hotel, the only one in Johannesburg in those days. There seems to have been enough capital available because as I mentioned, decor and furnishings were all of superior quality.

The hotel had 300 rooms and six superb suites, with the presidential suite a jewel on its own. The old guestbooks are full of names of famous and important personalities from all walks of life. Situated on top of the hotel was the nightclub, previously known as the 6,000 Club because the room was approximately 6,000 feet above sea level. The interior had been changed by a previous manager, causing it to lose all its splendour and attractiveness.

A swimming pool adjoined the coffee shop, which you found on the third floor. For banquets, we had the Gold Room, which could seat 500 persons with a number of smaller rooms for private parties.

In the basement, a disco catered for the younger generation and in the Medieval Hall a weekly medieval dinner was served on the similar lines you find in old castles in Ireland and Wales. These two venues were started with the hope of attracting additional revenue, as the hotel profits had started to decline. In my opinion, a wrong decision. Firstly, the disco, as mentioned above to attract a younger generation, could only be reached through the main entrance. Hotel guests relaxing in the lobby were disturbed by noisy and rowdy people passing by and on many occasions seating themselves in the lobby as well as driving away all others.

The Medieval Hall, although making some profit, also had to be approached through the main entrance. The menu included free wine, as much as you were able to consume. One of the highlights of the evening was when a guest was put in the stocks (a wooden construction where head and hands were placed between wooden planks). In medieval days you found those constructions in many towns and villages, market places and village greens. The people who were put in the stocks were mostly small criminals or other offenders against the law. They were then easy prey to be bombarded with rotten eggs and tomatoes. So in the Medieval Hall of the hotel, this resulted mainly in the poor person in the stocks being smothered with pieces of food and in other cases with wine being poured over him. In most cases, I was obliged to pay for the dry cleaning of the soiled clothes. What made me discontinue this special event, however, was when some drunken fools started shooting at the lights and chandeliers with their revolvers, which in any case should have been deposited with the security department before entering the hotel.

Since the opening of the President, other five-star hotels had been built in Johannesburg and when I took over three others were in evidence. The position, or rather the location, of the hotel was somewhat unfortunate as it stood next to the railway station, where thousands of Africans used to catch their trains and passed the hotel to do so. Every time there were some disturbances, they took place mostly around the station and the hotel.

Having special kitchens and equipment for the preparation of kosher food, we catered intensively for the Jewish community.

As far as I remember this was the only place I managed where you had to provide a sample menu for about six persons ahead of the function. OK, this was an accepted custom, but providing also wine, brandy and cigars free of charge really in my estimation took things a little too far. If you thought that was all, you had another matter awaiting you when it came to settle the bill, because there was always some kind of complaint about the food, and invariably a discount was asked for. The soup was too salty, the fish was not as ordered, the sweet too sweet and so on.

One incident really sticks in my mind. We decided to hold a New Year's Eve Ball, which had been quite successful some years back. However, the Carlton Hotel had been the scorer lately and had established quite a name for itself. So anyway, we wanted to have a go again. As the sale of tickets was not satisfactory, we were forced to cancel the function. Fortunately we took the precaution when we sold the tickets of asking for the telephone number or address of the purchaser. We were able to contact all except three people. We made bookings for these people at the Carlton and the sales manager had to approach the people on arrival and explain to them the situation and take them to the Carlton in his hotel car.

Two or three days later, I received a phone call from one of the parties, complaining that they did not enjoy the evening at the Carlton, that the whole affair was a mess-up. In the meantime, we contacted the other parties we booked at the Carlton; they both said they had a marvellous time and enjoyed it very much. To smooth things over, as I felt somewhat guilty, I invited them to the Transvaal Room for a free à la carte dinner, with wine and all the other trimmings. A day later one of their servants arrived with a letter demanding the ticket money back plus SA rand 600, for a dress that his wife specially bought for the occasion.

This I found going a bit too far and I informed them that the original offer still stood: a free meal at the Transvaal Room. Promptly I received another call with the threat to report the whole matter to the newspaper should I not accept their demands. As sometimes a bad report can be good advertising for a business, I told them to go ahead as I could well do with free advertising. Nothing ever appeared in the papers and my offer of a free dinner was never taken up.

Chapter Eleven

Bahrain

As with all Arabian states it is difficult, virtually impossible, to find local people to take on manual jobs and lower positions in the hotel trade.

So it was decided before taking up my position in Bahrain that I should proceed to Sri Lanka, as it is known today, and interview and sign up staff from our company hotel, the Pegasus Reef. I was looking forward to visiting the hotel again to see for myself the changes that had taken place over the years since my assignment there. So having handed over the President to my successor, Mavis and I boarded the plane for Colombo via the Seychelles.

We were met by the hotel manager at the airport and proceeded slowly to the hotel. The gardens looked beautiful and across the street from the hotel a number of souvenir shops had established themselves. Otherwise, there were no visual changes.

As I had contacted the manager a few weeks before with my intention of engaging staff for Bahrain, he had made it known to his own staff, so that I could proceed without much time being lost with the interviewing. It seemed that jobs abroad were very much in demand and I had many more applicants on the list than I really required. Most of the applying staff were known to me, which cut down the time set aside for the interviews. Consequently, we had time to visit our friends and look around Colombo, where real change had taken place. Many new hotels had opened, managed and run by international hotel chains. I caught a cold and the doctor refused permission for me to fly, as my ears were affected. So a few pleasant extended days were necessary.

After these few extra days, we flew on to Bahrain to have a look at my new assignment, getting to know the island and establish contact. This time we were met by the chairman of the company and chauffeured by Rolls-Royce to the hotel. Here our plans were for Mavis to fly to Switzerland and myself to London to head office for a few days before joining up at home. Due to a mistake by the booking office, we discovered that the plane that was to fly Mavis to Zurich no longer operated and the next available flight was two days later. When we wished to extend our stay we were informed the hotel was fully booked and we had to vacate on the date arranged. Not even talking to the manager had any effect, as accommodation at the hotel was overbooked and some of the guests slept in the hotel lounge as no rooms were available on the island. Luckily Mavis had the address of some old friends from our Jamaica days, now living in Bahrain, and after contacting them, they were very happy to have her spend the two nights with them in their flat. After that, we spent a couple of weeks at home, where we spent most of the time clearing our garden, which now looked like a jungle, and carrying out other repairs. The time passed very quickly and then, packing our three customary suitcases, we were off to another new assignment and island.

The company had two projects under construction in Bahrain, the seventy-bedroom commercial hotel Al Jazira in the old section of the city – with a small restaurant and bar – plus the 300-bedroom, five-star Diplomat Hotel on reclaimed land. As I mentioned, both hotels were still under construction, with the Al Jazira first in line. In charge was an American architect and we became friends in a very short time. I was open to new ideas and new hotel techniques, which made it easy to undertake changes on the original designs. This was quite refreshing as in the past I always found certain difficulties in persuading architects to make changes which were beneficial to the operation. Most of them seemed to concentrate on the public side and were not really interested in behind-the-scenes areas, where for the operator at least things could be made considerably easier for future operation.

Our first residence was at a local hotel owned and managed by a director of the company. Quite a character, but very helpful, his office looked more like a bric-a-brac shop than a place of work. He also owned a few houses outside the town. The area was surrounded by a three-metre-high wall with an entrance door that looked like a door in an old American fort in the Indian territories. All the executives involved in the construction of the new hotels were living there and we named the settlement, in accordance with its appearance, the Apache Fort. The gate was manned twenty-four hours a day and the door closed after 11 p.m. every day. The owner had his own residence at the Apache Fort, with the sole telephone for the whole community at his villa. The so-called swimming pool was still under construction, would be so for the next few years and probably still is today. Adjoining the owner's villa was the warehouse for the supermarket, also owned by him some way away. This was stocked with goods that would be sufficient to feed the local police force for a month. Some of the goods were already outdated, some of them by two years, but were still finding customers and sold at the supermarket at ever increasing prices.

To start with, there was the local souk, where anything you desired could be found. It was always very crowded, especially in the early evening hours when the immigrant workers finished their day's work. After closing time, rats and cockroaches took over, roaming freely around. It was not surprising as sanitary regulations did not exist, or they were ignored. It was not unusual when you took a walk through the narrow streets in the evening to be hit by chicken bones or other food items thrown out of the windows above. Just behind the Al Jazira was a chicken merchant. You bought a live bird at one side of the street, took it to the other side to have it killed, feathered and carried home to cook for dinner.

So at one side you had the old traditions with donkey carts, then through the narrow streets, the modern and expensive cars driving around the modern part of the town with elegant restaurants, nightclubs with international shows and other Western entertainment.

The whole island seemed to be a construction site with modern buildings going up all over the place, with at least six large luxury hotels in various stages of completion.

The date of the opening of the Al Jazira soon came around. Staff housing just outside the city was ready and the staff started to arrive as scheduled.

Our days at the Apache Fort were coming to an end and we moved to a suite at the hotel. Filling the rooms was no problem, as the room shortage on the island still existed. We enjoyed a good turnover in the restaurant and the introduction of a happy hour in the early evening in our small bar turned out to be a tremendous source of income for the hotel. One or two hotels tried to compete against us but were not very successful, which was very encouraging for us and showed once again when one is first with an idea and are successful, the client remains faithful although other hotels may copy.

The Diplomat's progress, although quite fast on our arrival, started to slow down and certain amenities had to be shelved due to financial difficulties. The Korean company in charge of the construction, however, maintained its complete labour force which consisted 100 per cent of Koreans managed under strict discipline, living in their own camp, even with girls imported from Korea to satisfy the sexual needs of the workers. A big controversy existed with the local business community as the Koreans even imported all the foodstuffs required to feed the workers. With the teething troubles over at the Al Jazira, I found more time to concentrate on the interior side of the Diplomat, especially as the project manager for the hotel had been withdrawn.

Bahrain, although an island, has few good beaches, with the exception of the Sheikh's beach, which has a nice sandy stretch on his private property. By kind permission, it is accessible to Europeans only. He has built himself a nice villa adjoining the beach and could be seen relaxing there on the terrace having tea and inviting visitors to join him. I never had the pleasure of being invited but Bernie did meet him and, according to discussion with the Sheikh, he knew of me and my activities, assignment and so on. Mavis and I did spend many pleasant hours on this beach although it was very hot during the summer months.

Once a month, an executive belonging to the project department visited us to see for himself the progress achieved. As it happened, we were unable to secure accommodation in a good hotel on one particular occasion and found as a last resort a room at the hotel we stayed in on our arrival a few months ago. He arrived late at night and was to attend a meeting the next day at 10 a.m. The appointed time passed without him present and after waiting for about half an hour we postponed the meeting until the afternoon. He was duly present this time and recounted the reason for his not being present in the morning: he overslept. Apparently, as he discovered when he woke up about midday, his room had no window; although curtains were closed on his arrival, when he opened them this morning he was looking at a blank wall.

Overhearing conversations at the bar I frequently heard the words 'white submarine'. According to the stories it seemed to be quite a lively place so naturally I wanted to know more.

Apparently my chairman had one on the grounds of his summer house (for the winter months he had another house, much more suitable for the cooler weather and near to Manama, the capital of Bahrain). Anyway to give his sons more freedom and a life of their own, he had constructed a large raised swimming pool with five fully furnished luxurious apartments underneath. It seems that these apartments were quite 'in' with the local European girls and airhostesses. Mavis and I were once invited by one of the sons to visit his flat and I must say to entice a young girl it had the right ambience, with subdued lighting, stereo music, a sunken bath and a nice cosy bar. Some people seem to have all the luck.

I think before proceeding further a few words should be said regarding the customs and traditions of the Middle East, which I had learned to observe. It was customary for me to visit the chairman's office twice a week. Formal announcement was not asked for, so I just went along when I had some spare time to report on business matters. Upon being invited to take a seat on the sofa next to his table, before any discussion took place Arabian tea was served by the servant, which you accepted in your right hand, taking small sips at a time. After the first cup, tea is again offered but according to custom you should never take more than three cups. Never cross your legs, apparently, and also never show the soles of your shoes. It quite often happens that the conversation ceases suddenly for a short period, so you are not to make any statement or comments until your host asks a question or makes a reply. It is quite in order that other people enter the office to discuss a problem while you are sitting also in the same room; you wait until the matter has been settled and you continue your conversation again. Sometimes I was there over an hour, although everything that was said could have been dealt with in ten minutes. It is impolite to leave until the host wishes you goodbye, a custom which I found quite educational and good sense. You may find that during a business conversation or meeting, a son of the family is usually present sitting next to his father, listening, observing but not saying a word. When I asked the chairman, I was informed that through this, the young man would learn how to deal with business, which should make him sufficiently mature to take over the business when the time arrives for the old man to retire.

Earlier on I mentioned that we experienced some financial trouble during the construction of the Diplomat. Considerable amounts were outstanding to some local suppliers, which prompted them to take action. So one morning when I was trying to enter the site, I was stopped by armed police, who prevented anyone from entering. No work was going on and was only resumed when the suppliers were paid and satisfied. Then a few months later a mysterious fire broke out at the office building on the site, destroying the accounts office. Needless to say, various rumours were circulating around town.

My friend the architect had to make frequent visits to London and as his wife was especially fond of cats, he decided to bring one back for her to Bahrain, and decided on a Persian type. He arrived back without the cat and revealed to me that he went to Harrods, selected a nice cat – not too cheap, either – purchased a basket for air transport and was about to pay for everything when the saleswoman flatly refused to complete the deal as the cat was going to an Arab country, with the remark that cats are not looked after properly there and many times are left behind as strays when the expatriate owners leave the island. He did in the end find a good-looking stray male cat locally and this cat must have been one of the most travelled animals, as it went with them everywhere.

Bahrain was quite fashionable for Saudis to visit for an enjoyable weekend, as alcohol and girls were freely available. The contents of a minibar were usually not sufficient to keep them happy and orders were given to room service to provide full bottles instead of miniatures. I do recall that some of them never left the room for the whole weekend, just drinking and enjoying themselves. In all fairness, it must be said that we never had any trouble and no liquor was bought outside and brought into the hotel. This could have been done at one third of the price paid to us.

The way it looked, the immigrant workers seemed to out-number the Bahrainis. They were mostly from India, Pakistan and Bangladesh. Their living quarters were a disgrace, with twenty to thirty crammed into a small room. During the summer months, most of them slept outside on flat roofs on top of the buildings. Such a place was just approximately ten metres from the hotel and when I climbed on to the hotel roof, I was able to watch. I must have counted more than 100 persons being accommodated in this way.

Although the government demanded a minimum salary from the Arab employer of 140 dinars per month, with food and lodging, many of the workers never received this amount once they arrived.

To cut these wages, the employer informed the workers after they had been working for a few weeks that their standard of work was not satisfactory and they had to return home, where poverty and hunger awaited them. Consequently they were quite prepared to accept a much lower wage just to remain in the country and in employment. Apart from myself, the only other European executive was the assistant manager, a Cypriot, the housekeeper, a thorough German woman, and the chef, who came from Switzerland.

We were a well-geared team and had the workforce com-pletely behind us, which gave the hotel a good standing in competition with other and larger hotels on the island. British Airways accorded us the status of 'British Airways-Appointed Hotel' for Bahrain and we did receive a number of requests, especially from service clubs who wanted to use the hotel, but regretfully we could not accept, as we had no separate facilities such as banquet rooms and so on to accommodate them. In the meantime, rather lengthy negotiations took place between the owning company and the banks to overcome the financial problems. Work at the site of the Diplomat had come virtually to a standstill. The Korean contractor withdrew most of his labour force and the architect, having become very frustrated, left also. Although the Al Jazira, originally intended as an office building and then converted into a hotel, made good profit, large enough after the high rent of over 20,000,000 dinars per month, it could not in the eyes of the company warrant our carrying on as a hotel. So eventually the hotel ceased to operate after a few months.

I left the island for Riyadh to open the Riyadh Palace Hotel.

The banks in Bahrain eventually offered to meet the required money to complete the Diplomat – but the long delay cost the hotel dearly as by now a number of large hotels had opened their doors and established themselves. The shortage of hotel accommodation had now been reversed, as suddenly plenty was available.

Chapter Twelve

Saudi Arabia

Although the principle and the basis of managing hotels is the same all over the world, there are of course some local traditions and customs that do influence the day-to-day management.

This applies especially to Saudi Arabia.

The Saudis' way of life, their religious beliefs, are very strong factors that also affect the hotel industry.

For a newcomer, it is quite a change and takes a little time to adapt to the new conditions and requirements.

Islam has a very strong influence on the nation and it is therefore not surprising that nearly all laws, rules and regulations are governed by its influence.

The sale and consumption of alcohol is strictly forbidden. The words 'beer', 'wine' and 'spirit' are not admissible, so non-alcoholic beer becomes malt beverage and non-alcoholic wine becomes grape beverage.

All meats are allowed, with the exception of pork. As a substitute for pork bacon, beef bacon is available on the market but as the word 'bacon' is connected with pork, this is printed on the menu as 'breakfast beef'.

When we were preparing our à la carte menu for the restaurants, we took the precaution of having them checked first by a local expert, but had to make a number of changes. Soufflé Rothschild was out, because of the Jewish connection. The word 'Copacabana' was not allowed because it represented a famous nightclub. The whole structure of the menu presented quite a problem. Traditional French dishes had to be omitted, as we did not have the wines to cook the dish according to the recipe.

I recall the incident when one manager advertised in the daily English newspaper a special menu for Thanksgiving with Saudi champagne included. Now, everyone in Saudi knew that Saudi champagne consisted of apple juice mixed with Perrier water and a few slices of orange and lemon. However, because the word 'champagne' was used in an advertisement, the manager was promptly arrested and jailed.

Television covers the whole country, but the programmes are all in Arabic, with the exception of daily news coverage in English.

To provide some entertainment for the foreign hotel residents, the hotel provided in-house video. Videos were readily available in Riyadh. Most of the films were suitable for private viewing but not for the hotels where religious rules were strictly applied.

Girls in bathing costumes, kissing and cuddling were definitely out, and so were any films with religious themes.

To satisfy the authorities, I installed two video sets in my apartment and my wife had the job of viewing a film, noting the offending parts and producing a new video suitable for the hotel. In many cases, the film had to be abandoned, as after elimination of the offending scenes, the film lost its meaning.

In the beginning, most videos were smuggled into the country and were recordings from either the BBC or ITV. Some still had the advertisements on the tape, even the British weather reports.

Fairly regularly, new instructions were received and new regulations with the compliments of the religious government.

'You are herewith requested to place a direction sign for Mecca in every room,' was one request. We decided to produce a round plastic plate with an arrow in the middle with the word 'Mecca' in English and Arabic on either side. The maintenance staff were then handed a compass, which showed the direction of Mecca, wherever one might be standing in the world. So far so good, until one day when I received a visit from an Arabian hotel guest. He was very polite and told me that the direction signs in the rooms were very useful and very appreciated, but unfortunately the direction arrow was pointing in the wrong direction. Without delay, I informed the maintenance department, who confirmed the client's complaint. Apparently the signs were installed next to the telephone and the metal within the set affected the needle of the compass. The mistake was corrected immediately and I was glad that the hotel guest did not take the matter too seriously. I could have easily ended up in jail if the matter had been reported to the authorities.

You do hear a lot of strange and not always encouraging stories about Saudi Arabia, but Mavis and I enjoyed our three years there.

Agreed, life is somewhat demanding for women, not being allowed to drive a car, use the hotel swimming pools or wear European dress when visiting town. They did, however, find their own ways to enjoy and entertain themselves.

Running the hotel was not always easy; you were breaking the local laws to some extent nearly every day. Landing in jail was always at the back of your mind.

Like a newborn child, a new hotel needs nursing along until it reached maturity. The Riyadh Palace was no exception.

An influential Saudi Arabian journalist booked a suite about two weeks after the opening and did not find everything at the hotel to his satisfaction, which prompted him to write an article in the national Arab newspaper. I was made aware of this fact by my chairman during my weekly meeting with him. As one always learns from mistakes, I took the necessary action to correct the mentioned shortcomings in the article without delay.

Roughly two months later I met the writer of the article in a shop in town. After greeting him, I mentioned the fact that we had not had the pleasure of seeing him at the hotel for quite some time.

'I thought you wouldn't accept me any longer since I made my report in the paper,' was his reply.

I went on to explain to him that we were grateful for the comments, which gave us the opportunity to improve our service, and that he was always welcome at the hotel. Some time later he did check in again at the hotel and called me to his suite, complimenting me on the improvements and at the same time presented me with a gold coin, expressing his appreciation. Needless to say, we became quite friendly and had lengthy discussions on the hotel business, relating espe-cially to Saudi Arabia, which he did reflect in various articles in his newspaper.

Other countries, other customs. This applies especially to Saudi Arabia. Sending a bill to a creditor for payment through the post is not known here and you may wait for ever for your money. To collect the outstanding debt, the hotel has to employ so-called debt collectors.

We had two such persons on our staff and discovered that one of them, a Moroccan, had been lining his own pocket with some of the money. A court sentenced him to six months in jail. A short time before his term of sentence was completed I was invited to meet the judge in charge of the case. After the usual small talk, the fate of the prisoner was discussed, which meant I had to make a decision on three proposals.

Firstly, the sentence was to be extended for another six months.

Secondly, we have his right hand cut off for the offence.

Thirdly, we send him back to his own country and hand him over to the police there to decide what further action should be taken against him.

I must say, I was taken aback by this turn of events, especially as it was left to me to make my judgement on this man. Without much hesitation, I informed the judge to apply the third option and send the man home.

Years later, during a stay in Morocco, I met the man quite by chance on the streets of Agadir and was very happy to learn that on his return from Saudi, no further punishment was forthcoming from the local authorities, apart from a stern warning to stay out of trouble.

Weddings are quite important occasions in Saudi Arabia, like everywhere else in the world. Most weddings take place approximately six weeks before the months of Ramadan. A wedding cake of up to ten tiers is not unusual and is in most cases produced by the hotel's pastry cook.

After the photos of the happy couple cutting the cake had been taken, the cake was, unknown to me, removed without delay by the pastry chef. I only got wind of this when towards the end of the so-called wedding season, a father of the bride complained that the cake was so hard that it could not be cut and when I asked the chef to check it out, was informed that after every wedding the pastry cook iced the bottom layer and used it again for the next wedding.

Considering the price of the cake, which ranged between

R2,000 to 3,000, I was not surprised to see a good kitchen result.

Right from the opening day of the hotel, our suites were heavily booked, mostly by rich Saudis. I learned later that every manager of a newly opened hotel had experienced this. Maybe it was some kind of a thrill to the Arab to sample the suites of a new hotel. Anyway, whatever the reason, we did a good business with our suites, which were not very cheap in price.

One afternoon I received a call from the telephonist that the occupant of suite 601 wanted to see me urgently. On entering the suite, I found one of my telephonists in the sitting room, together with the occupant who had bloodstained clothing. The guest complained that he was punched on the nose by my telephonist. Naturally, I wanted to know the reason and was told that the guest had sold a Rado watch to the telephonist for R2,000, which was found to be a fake when examined by a local jeweller. The telephonist confronted the guest in his suite, demanding his money back, which was refused, prompting the blow to the face.

I immediately asked myself how this guest was going to settle his bill if he was trying to sell a fake watch to one of my employees, so I just asked him this question. Without hesitation he admitted he did not have the required funds and for this reason he was selling this watch. He swore he did not know it was a fake.

On checking with the reception, I was informed that his bill amounted to R6,000. As he had no guarantee or other means to settle the bill, I had no other choice than to have him arrested.

A few days later, the police wanted to know what further steps I would propose to take in this case. I called the telephonist to my office to discuss the matter, as I have learned over the years that the local people know much better how to deal with a situation like this than a foreigner.

'Leave the matter to me,' he said. 'Just you give me the permission to take over the problem.'

'How are you going about it?' I wanted to know.

'First of all, I will ask the police to hand over the prisoner to me together with a policeman and then we will visit friends and relations of the man in Riyadh, explain the case to them and ask for a contribution to settle his debt with the hotel and for me to recover the R2,000,' was the reply.

'OK by me and good luck,' I said.

About four or five hours later, he returned with the news that the collected money amounted to roughly R6,000. Since no more friends and relations were available, he would find some other way to collect the rest.

Late afternoon, he called again at my office with the news that he was short of R600 owed to both of us.

'How did you get this money together?' I wanted to know.

'Oh, quite easy. I made the man sit down on a busy street corner and when a passer-by wanted to know why the man was sitting there and crying, I explained and some of them handed me some money to help him.'

I had to laugh. I told him to forget the outstanding amount and have the police release the man.

'No chance! I want my money,' he replied, 'and I will take him again to a street corner.'

However, not ten minutes passed before he returned with a satisfied grin on his face, telling me that all the money had been collected. This came about because the Arab sold his genuine Rado watch for R700 to the policeman who was accompanying them as a guard. Honestly, I would never thought or have dreamt of getting the money together in this way.

Getting married in Saudi is quite a different affair than in Europe. The actual wedding takes place at home within a small family circle. For other relations, friends and acquaintances, parties are arranged that are male and female only, that is, no woman is allowed to attend a male party and vice versa.

As weddings usually take place prior to the holy month of Ramadan, the hotels are usually heavily booked. We were mostly in demand for the female parties. The set-up of the hall was usually the same, consisting of banquet-theatre seating with a dance floor and space for a large female band consisting mostly of drums for the entertainment. The requirements for the banquet could be quite varied inasmuch as the client might wish to have their own staff looking after the party, to have the hotel lit up outside with strings of white lights, with a five- to fifteen-tier wedding cake, their own choice of menu and a raised platform with two upholstered easy chairs for the bridal couple. All of this is discussed at length, a price agreed upon and a down payment of at least twenty per cent is demanded by the hotel.

In all cases I can recall, the organiser insisted that his own servants or a local contractor prepare the Arabic coffee and tea that is served during the celebrations. The organisers arrive about an hour before the party, bringing along their own cooking equipment, which consists mostly of charcoal burners, serving pots and crockery. About 8 p.m. the women start arriving in their chauffeur-driven cars clothed in couturier dresses and jewels; diamonds and not gold. On entering the banqueting hall, they remove the local covering dress and the room looks like any party in Europe, with elegantly dressed women mingling together. Because being Christian and considered infidels by the Muslim religion, hotel staff, providing they are not Muslim, are allowed to go about their duties. I must say, I was on many occasions astonished by the expensive and latest fashions from Europe the women were wearing and some of them were quite stunning beauties, not only in dress but in figure.

By now the band would have started to play, coffee and tea and Turkish delight would have been served and some women would have started to dance, while others looked on or chatted away with each other. Around midnight the groom would appear sitting himself and his bride on the bridal chairs on the raised platform to receive good wishes accompanied by a small envelope or another gift from the invited guests.

Once the last well wishers had been received, the couple would proceed to cut the cake. The top tier would be removed, cut into small pieces and served to the guests, during which time the groom would leave to join his own party. The festivities would continue as before until 2 or 3 a.m., when the banquet would be served. All the food would be placed on the extra-wide tables with seats on either side. Everyone would take their seat, and help themselves to the food on the table. Within a half hour or so the banquet would be finished and the party would start breaking up.

Although we did not receive many complaints, we had to accept certain customs, such as that about one third of the food available on the banquet table had to be left behind, otherwise there would be some complaints that there was not enough food. Or when own staff were provided, which were mostly women bringing along their babies and small children, the little ones, after the banquet, were placed on the banqueting table to fill their stomachs, while their mothers collected the remaining food in large plastic bags to take home.

However, I had a complaint towards the end of the wedding season that could have resulted in considerable trouble for the person involved and the hotel itself. It concerned one of my executives. Apparently, according to my senior security officer, the food and beverage manager was seen entering a hotel bedroom with a local Arabian girl attending the wedding party the previous night. When I called the man involved to my office, he admitted the charges. In his version, he was approached by a girl, wanting to know if there were empty rooms available at the hotel and he replied with the number. She invited him to take her to one of them, and having been starved of women's company for a number of months, he enjoyed a happy hour with her.

Aware of the serious consequences if the girl's family got wind of the affair, I asked him to pack his bags and be available to leave the country as soon as I could obtain an exit visa for him from the immigration department. Although it did take at least a few days to obtain such a document through my contacts, I was able to fly him out the same evening and, I must say, just in the nick of time, as the next day I received a visit from the girl's brother demanding to see the already departed culprit. What kind of action he wanted to take is still unclear to me today. Contacting the police would have been quite out of the question, because if this instance got around in certain circles, the girl's reputation and chances of a good match would have been ruined.

Chapter Thirteen

England

After nearly three years in Saudi, head office decided to transfer me to London for a while until such time as a new assignment was found for me.

Mavis returned to our home in Switzerland and I was asked to attend one or two seminars in England to bring me up to date with changed management methods. As quite considerable leave was due to me, I went to join Mavis at home to await further developments. One morning the personnel manager of the company came on the phone with a request to help him out, as he needed a manager for a small hotel in Somerset rather urgently. Naturally if I was not interested in running a small place with a dozen or so rooms, two bars and a small restaurant he would understand, but he was in rather a tight spot and would be very happy if I would agree. The assignment would only be for three or four weeks, but in actual fact turned out to be more than three months.

Anyway, off I went to run a nice old country hotel in Dunster. I must say, I was in for quite a shock, after running large hotels for so many years. Apart from myself, there were two reception-ists, a chef with two helpers, one barman and head waiter and three waitresses-come-chambermaids on the regular staff, with one or two extras who came to help out at weekends.

So I found myself at the reception in the morning, placing orders, taking deliveries, and selling and serving drinks in the restaurant during lunch and dinner, relieving the barman during his mealtimes and stocking up the bar and helping out in the bar during the evenings when necessary. Before retiring, which was never before 11.30 p.m., I had to make a tour of the hotel and switch off all unnecessary lights, and close all the doors and windows, so believe me, after such a hard day, I was ready for bed. I prayed that all guests were in bed and that I did not have to get up when they arrived late to open the door or that nobody called on the phone with some silly request.

On the barman's day off, I had to run the bars, which I quite enjoyed. There was the normal public bar with a large fireplace and the private bar where mostly Somerset cider was served. Each regular client had his own mug, which he left permanently in the bar. So you can imagine, I sometimes served, especially in the beginning, the cider in the wrong mug. But I must say, they took it in good humour and we had many a good laugh together.

Mind you, they knew their cider and when it was not up to standard they refused to drink it.

Every Sunday morning before opening time, I had to clean the beer and cider pipes and pumps and rewind at least a dozen old clocks, each with its separate key, climbing on stools to reach them.

Don't ask me what happened but one particular evening, but without any reason whatsoever, I rang the closing bell in the bar one hour too early to the great astonishment of the guests, for which they forgave me immediately. But it must have been the talk of the village for days, because I was reminded probably a hundred times of my mistake during the next two weeks.

I always thought English food was plain and unimaginative but I changed my mind after a spell in Somerset. The dishes the chef produced, which were mostly local, were not only good and appetising but also very enjoyable. For my part, I really enjoyed them and, as I said, changed my mind for ever about English food.

The hotel must have been at least 600 years old and was originally inhabited by monks. It had a kind of character and atmosphere that can only be found in England, Wales, Scotland and Ireland.

I do not recall having many days off work apart from a short visit to Somerset, a trip to London to sort out some business matters and of course three days in Switzerland to attend my son's wedding. I did manage to have some short walks into the countryside and visit the nearby town of Minehead during the twice-weekly banking of the daily takings. What really surprised me again and again was the friendliness and acceptance of a foreigner like me without reserve or hesitation. I recall my time as assistant manager in Leamington where the people were more reserved and it took about three months until they acknowledged me as part of the hotel. There it was my duty to close the bars every night and only about a month later a regular guest of the bar wanted to know who I was. Before that they were ignorant of my greetings.

But back to Dunster where I really got into the swing of things. The work was very tiring and I think it must have shown on my features because I was also the hotel porter, and as the hotel had no parking facilities and the hotel garage, which originally was the horse stables, could not be used any more, I had to sometimes carry the luggage short distances. Some of the guests must have felt sorry for me because they insisted that they carry the luggage themselves; more generally they were of the opinion I was the hotel porter and placed many a tip in my hands.

They were very surprised when I refused to accept and told them I was the innkeeper.

Anyway, the weeks passed quickly and I still have fond memories of the time spent there.

Oh, I nearly forgot to mention that I decided to grow a beard during my holidays, much to the objection of Mavis, who was very reluctant to kiss me, as she did not like the prickling of the hair. So when I left Dunster for a good rest in Switzerland, I decided to cut off my beard there and then in the train between Zurich and Chur. I got hold of my shaving gear and retired to the train toilet to carry out the task, which must have taken a good twenty minutes to accomplish. I looked quite funny when I viewed myself in the mirror because I was quite sunburned and where the beard was before, a white area looked at me. Anyway Mavis was quite happy, despite my funny look, for having done away with the beard. For myself, I was somewhat sad because in a way I was quite proud of it and thought a beard fitted me nicely.

Ireland

After my well-earned holidays, I reported back to London, where my next assignment was spelled out to me. My task was to go to

Ireland, visit the company's hotels there and put together a business plan with the local manager. Generously, the company agreed that Mavis could accompany me. So off we went, first to the airport hotel in Dublin, then onwards to Ennis and Kinsale. I had never been to Ireland before and was looking forward to meeting the Irish face to face. The only experience I had with them dated back many years when I found them working in kitchens and other departments in the hotels in England. I was quite thrilled by their attitude to life and their sense of humour.

We learnt all about Ireland's history from the taxi driver who drove us from Ennis to Kinsale. The roads were narrow and very winding, cutting through lovely green countryside. How he got us safely to Kinsale is still a puzzle to me. There he was, driving along, sitting sideways in the driver's seat, looking at us, talking all the time about Ireland and only glancing at the road out the corner of his eye.

We heard a lot about Kinsale all around Ireland, as it is quite well known for its various restaurants and good food. Unfortunately, most of them were closed, as it was nearly winter when we arrived there. But we were determined to find out if the name lived up to the reputation and I must confess we were not disappointed and really enjoyed the local food served to us. Most of the restaurants are family run and must be quite profitable because we were told that the owners make enough profit during the summer season to afford to spend the winter months in warmer climates, such as in Spain, Portugal and even the Caribbean.

After completing my task, we returned to Dublin to the airport hotel, awaiting new instructions, which were not long in coming. I was to proceed to Belfast to take over the hotel until a new manager arrived. We decided to take the train between Dublin and Belfast. Not a very long journey, but a bit risky as the IRA sometimes blew up the rails. Anyhow, we waved away the warnings and decided to take the risk. It turned out to be a nice enjoyable trip with afternoon tea served in each compartment by a waiter wearing white gloves.

Arriving at Belfast station, I was surprised to hear our name called over the public address system, asking us to report to the information office. Once there we were informed that owing to a slight hitch, learnt from an executive of the company, the arrangements had been changed for the time being and we were asked to return to Dublin. So off we went back to Dublin on the same train we arrived on a short while before. Three days later we did the same journey again and this time no message awaited us at the station and we proceeded as scheduled to the hotel.

Of course we were aware of the Troubles in Northern Ireland but never expected to find the hotel surrounded by a six-foot wire fence and barbed wire, with a checkpoint manned by armed security guards, checking your luggage and searching your body for hidden weapons. At first it was quite a shock, but after a while you got used to the situation, being checked when entering government buildings, hotels, shops and shopping areas.

Despite the Troubles the hotel enjoyed a good occupancy from business people. We stayed there for about ten weeks until the new manager arrived, but did not see much of Northern Ireland as the weather during the winter months was not very inviting and when the spring started to show its signs we were off again. In a sense, we were not sorry to leave as the whole situation of the Troubles could be very trying at certain times and somewhat wearing.

Manchester

I was longing to join the international division again and go abroad, but as there were no vacancies immediately, the Grand Hotel in Manchester was offered to me and I accepted.

The Grand is one of the oldest hotels in Manchester and was built over one hundred years ago. Like all hotels of this kind, they have a hard time competing against the newcomers and more modern properties.

What was really difficult for me was to adapt myself to the new ways of management. In the past, I had much more respon-sibility and was in many ways my own boss and decision-maker. Now I found a lot of things were decided by people above me and that therefore the work became monotonous. I found it hard to accept the new situation and found myself hitting against a wall when I wanted something changed.

The day arrived when something of a solution had to be found for my problems. I requested a transfer to the international division but without success and after some lengthy discussions I decided to leave the company after fifteen years with them. I made a lot of very good friends, but also a lot of enemies, which is unavoidable in everyone's life. I did enormously enjoy my years as general manager and it was with a heavy heart when I left for good.

So, as I had to remain at Manchester after tendering my resignation until such time as a new manager was appointed, we decided that Mavis should return home and prepare the house, as we did not know how long we would be living there. Naturally I did apply to various employment agencies for suitable vacancies and two days before I left Manchester I received a call to attend an interview in London in the next three days. On the same day the company invited me to a farewell dinner at a London hotel. Before the dinner, I attended the interview and secured a position as general manager in Cape Town with a starting date as soon as the necessary permits were ready for us to leave. I phoned the good news to Mavis and our long stay in Lüen, as had been anticipated, dwindled down to four weeks.

Cape Town

The twenty-five-storey four-star hotel in the suburb of Cape Town was completely refurbished with a number of non-smoking rooms, and a specially arranged room for executive females. At the top of the hotel was a revolving restaurant with an unrivalled panorama.

The top management formed a very experienced team, all with extensive knowledge of the hotel industry. Included in the hotel complex was a large entertainment area, which was closed.

New to me was a complete computer nerve centre of an accounting system, designed to provide ease of access to any account details required. It took nearly twenty minutes every day to go through the report, which consisted of thirty pages of two double-size A4 forms. The information contained was very detailed and informative, something like Big Brother. The nerve centre was fully air conditioned with large electronic equipment, and was only accessible to the specially trained staff who had a special coded card to enter. All the equipment was on a three-hour standby unit in case of power failure. When I think back, this was something out of this world for a hotel.

We enjoyed our stay in Cape Town. Seapoint is the entertainment section of Cape Town. The choice of restaurants and bars was enormous, with specialities from all over the world. The beaches and vineyards plus the easy life made it a very enjoyable place to stay.

Unfortunately, the turnaround for the hotel did not come up to expectations, maybe because of its past reputation. The reason for our departure just over one year later was first down to interference on the part of the owner, but also the South African law that foreigners have to reveal overseas assets after twelve months' stay. On the whole, the time we spent in the Cape will always remain as a very enjoyable period.

Chapter Fourteen

China

A few days after we arrived back at our home in Lüen, I received a telegram from a colleague I worked with in designing a hotel in Bahrain asking me if I would be interested in joining him as director of operations for a new hotel company operating in China, and if so, would I contact his office in California as he was currently in China. After talking this proposition over with my wife I telexed my acceptance. A week or so later, final arrangements were made through telexes and lengthy overseas cables to Hong Kong and the USA, and I was to fly to Hong Kong at the beginning of December, with a visit to China for approximately ten days, with the promise that I would be back for Christmas in Switzerland. While trying to make a booking with the airlines, I was to find out that most flights were fully booked and I had no other choice than to fly first class. I must say it was quite an experience and I made the most of it.

Collecting my luggage at the arrival terminal in Hong Kong, I took a taxi to the hotel, where I opened my case to find out that it didn't belong to me. It was an identical case with the same key to fit the lock. A quick dash to the airport was too late, as my case could not be found. In desperation, I went to the lost and found bureau, which was quite a job to locate, and was relieved to find my own luggage. After completing a lengthy document, with a lot of – in my opinion – silly questions, I returned, relieved, to the hotel.

The next day I tried to contact the Hong Kong office without success; either I had the wrong number or something else was wrong. The next day I was contacted by them and was told that they had problems with the telephone installation, but somebody would call around at the hotel for my passport to obtain a visa for China and the flight ticket. However, it would take about two or three days to complete this task, so why not have a look around Hong Kong? That is what I did and I was certainly impressed. I made some phone calls to old friends and arranged to meet them on my return from China. On my return to the hotel after an exhausting day of sightseeing in Hong Kong, the next day I found my passport and airline ticket waiting for me. I was to fly CAAC to Peking in two days' time.

A short flight of two hours brought me to Peking (now known as Beijing) towards the evening. Service on the plane was not to the standard I experienced on Western Airlines, but I must give credit to the hostesses, who tried their best. Custom formalities are lengthy at Peking Airport and it took about two hours until I met my friend waiting for me. We checked in at the Peking Grand Hotel, where the company rented an office. I must say, I was pleasantly surprised at the comfort of the bedroom with private bath, radio, telephone, an empty minibar and electrically operated curtains. I was told that the hotel was under Chinese management, had about 800 rooms and was originally built by the Russians. The new section, where I stayed, was built by a French company.

After dinner in an enormous dining room, I retired early to be woken up about midnight to pay for a phone call I had made earlier from my room. I then found out that, except for the bill for the room, everything else had to be paid for in cash and only in special tourist money, so-called Monopoly money.

The next day we undertook a tour of the city in the morning, visited the Friendship shop, which incidentally one finds in every major city. This shop was only for foreign visitors and only accepted tourist currency. The goods on offer included Chinese antiques, souvenirs, clothing and a considerable amount of Chinese medicine. In the afternoon, we visited the Fragrant Hill Hotel, approximately twenty kilometres from Peking, situated in a national park. The 270-bedroom luxury hotel built in 1982 was designed by the Chinese-American architect Im Pei combining Western comfort with traditional Chinese architecture. Like all new hotels in Peking the Fragrant Hill offers all the modern facilities you expect to find in a luxury hotel. It boasts a lovely garden with waterfalls, small lakes and invites you to dream the day away. The hotel, although only a few years old, needed attention and proper maintenance and appeared very much neglected. This was a very common factor that I found throughout my stay in China, where hotels were managed by Chinese. They just lacked the know-how of maintaining a hotel. One of the reasons we visited the hotel was because the owners were looking for a Western company to manage their hotel. It was really a shame to see such a lovely hotel going to pieces. Much of the modern machinery was in need of repair. The central air conditioning was so noisy due to lack of maintenance that you were unable to enjoy a good night's sleep.

On our way back to Peking, we discussed our plans for the next few days and it was decided that I should sample all the major hotels in Peking and pick the brains of the managers to obtain as much information as possible.

What surprised me in all the hotels I stayed in that were managed by Westerners was the high standard of service and the friendliness and efficiency of the Chinese staff. The food was excellent and the cleanliness throughout the hotels beyond reproach. So, after about a week in Peking, Bill and I boarded the plane for Hong Kong. As mentioned earlier, the service on CAAC left much to be desired but this time, I think, they surpassed themselves; breakfast, which consisted of an omelette with rice, was served frozen.

We stayed in Hong Kong for two days, during which time I met the other company executives and left for home to celebrate Christmas with my family. Before leaving, I signed a contract and expected to return within the next two months. The company I joined was a large construction concern whose aims were to construct and manage hotels in China. Two contracts were already signed: one for Xian and the other in Tianjin.

One thing that one notices in China is the absence of motorcars on the road, but really one is overcome by the number of bicycles. Most cars on the road are taxis and it is quite difficult to get a taxi during the rush hour. The taxi we hired to take us to Fragrant Hill never exceeded forty kilometres an hour. Every time he reached this speed, the driver cut the motor, waited until the meter dropped to between ten and fifteen kilometres per hour and then started the engine again. As we could not converse with the driver, we never knew the reason for this. Probably he wanted to save petrol.

My return to China and Hong Kong was delayed until the end of March. However, I had enough to work on at home to set up company policy and procedure guidelines. On arrival in Hong Kong in March, my first task was to install myself in the company offices. A friend from the old days in Uganda now established in Hong Kong introduced me to some very good contacts in the hotel trade with extensive knowledge of China. Through them I gained a very good overall picture of what to expect. As my chief spent most of his time in China chasing contracts, I concentrated myself on preparing staff schedules, pre-opening budgets and so on. After about two weeks in Hong Kong, I was called to Peking to participate in the discussions for the possibility of taking over the management of the Fragrant Hill. The course of the various meetings that took place during the duration of a few days is rather strange to a Western mind and can be described as follows.

The first day, on arrival at the hotel, we were met not by the general manager but by the assistant manager, accompanied by a translator, who took us on a tour of the hotel. In the billiard room we found members of the staff enjoying a game of snooker; in the hairdressing room, the hairdresser fast asleep in one of the chairs. The kitchen was in need of a good cleaning, fridges were broken, only half of the laundry was working and the carpets in the corridors were full of small or large spots from spilled goods. The service in the restaurant was nearly non-existent and the waiters were eating in front of the client. It was a real pity that such a lovely hotel was allowed to be ruined by lack of management. After having paid for our own lunch and the coffee we had upon arrival, we left in the early afternoon without having been introduced to anyone else.

We returned the next day with our translator and were welcomed by the chief accountant and his assistant. They started by asking questions about the company as a whole and enquired what we had in mind as to how to turn the hotel around. We were quite open and explained to them our views and how we would approach the problems.

When our turn came to ask questions, they were very tight-lipped and were not prepared to open the books to us. The only information we were able to obtain was that the hotel employed 750 staff, which we found quite staggering. With an occupancy of between 250 and 300, we suggested reducing the staff to between 250 and 300. This was quite impossible, according to them, and furthermore the government would strongly object.

The only sector where savings could be made was in security. At the time there were 160 persons employed in that particular department and a reduction of around one hundred was possible.

After the lengthy meeting, we were taken on a tour of the staff quarters, which were situated about ten minutes from the hotel and which consisted of two large blocks of housing, one for single persons and the other for married couples and families.

The apartments and rooms were adequately furnished and quite comfortable. All the apartments had private bathrooms. A restaurant catered for the off-duty staff, including families. Next to the housing complex was a kindergarten, which catered for children where both parents were working. I must confess I did not expect such a high standard for staff. There are many countries in the West where staff are offered greatly inferior accommodation and standards.

On our way back to Peking, passing through new high-rise apartment blocks under construction, we were surprised to find that the Chinese used the prefabricated approach.

The translator, who did not accompany us to visit the staff quarters, informed us that the assistant accountant had told him that we were the tenth Western company trying to negotiate a management contract with the owners of the hotel.

The day being Friday, we did not return for further negotiations until the following Tuesday, when we were offered tea on arrival and taken to a posh meeting room, which was not shown to us on our tour. After a while we were joined by the executives we had met previously and the general manager of the hotel.

After the customary small talk, we sat down to more serious business. This time they presented us with their conditions for a contract. It was translated to us in English as the contract was written in Chinese. We did not commit ourselves at this stage and asked for a week to consider and to present our own recommendations and conditions.

The next day we telexed the contents of the contract to our office in Hong Kong, to have them translated into English by a competent authority. Two days later we had it returned. Right from the outset, when we first examined the contract we were quite puzzled by certain clauses and this was now confirmed. Without going into details, these had to be changed before we entered into an agreement. So off we went again. This time we were told they were not able to meet us before 9 p.m. As usual we hired a taxi to take us to the hotel. Luckily we allowed an hour more to reach there, and quite rightly so. Cars are not allowed to use their headlights, only maybe occasionally for two or three seconds to warn cyclists on the road that the car requires right of way. Bicycles in China have no lights or reflectors on the back and we had three or four small accidents on the road, each time without any injuries or serious damages. Anyway, with the speed we travelled, it was quite impossible to cause anything more serious than an angry protest by the cyclist.

The same delegation met us at the hotel and we sat down right away to serious business. We presented our case, making it quite clear that certain clauses in the proposed contract were not acceptable to us without certain adjustments. At the same time, we presented them with a list of expatriate staff requirements and a guideline of the required local staff to manage the hotel efficiently. We finished the meeting at about 10.30 p.m. and had dinner in the Chinese restaurant, which was neither bad nor good. Before leaving, we were told by the assistant manager that they would contact us again once they had studied our proposals.

After about ten days, we did receive a letter regretting that our proposed changes were not acceptable to them and they had decided to continue the management of the hotel on their established pattern.

With no other business to keep us in China, Bill and I booked a morning flight to Hong Kong. Economy class being fully booked, we made the flight in first class. Breakfast was served approximately half an hour after takeoff, which consisted of coffee, rolls, an omelette and rice with mushrooms. The omelette dish was, as before, half frozen, so we drank about six cups of coffee to fill our stomachs. Nearer home, we were served a choice of drinks with some nuts, plus a tie as a souvenir.

Straight from the airport to the office, we tried to find accommodation for the next few weeks. Being high season, this wasn't easy. Through the assistance of our travel agent we were able to find a room at the Lee Gardens for two nights only. These rooms were available only because the agent's allotment for a particular tour at the hotel was not complete. However, this tour was to move on in two days and for that reason the agent could not guarantee rooms, should the new tour be complete. As it turned out, we had to move out and we found a small room at the Hong Kong Hotel across the harbour in Kowloon. We left most of our luggage at the Lee Gardens for safekeeping, as we hoped to return shortly. No such luck; the Hong Kong Hotel informed us we would have to vacate the room after only two nights. Back to the travel agent to help who found rooms in two different hotels. Bill being the more senior executive, he took the room at the New World Hotel and I went to a hotel in Hong Kong Island which was something between a middle and low-class hotel. Every morning there was a tramp sitting outside the hotel entrance. His clothes would have stood up on their own if he had ever taken them off. His face and hands hadn't seen any soap or water for months. It was difficult to determine if he was Chinese, Western or a mixture of both. He didn't bother anybody and seemed to be content with life.

By now I had been over two months away from home and so far had not received any salary. Bill told me it would be forthcoming within the next few days and if not then definitely by next month. To save some money, I started to use the tram to get to work. This is about the cheapest transport in Hong Kong and I used to like to travel on the upper deck and watch the people and goings-on from above.

Many times I used to walk, especially after Bill and I were able to move back to Lee Gardens, and the distance from the office was not too far. If you have ever been to Hong Kong, you must have been bewildered by the sheer number of people. Walking fast and overtaking on the sidewalks is impossible. Some of the shop signs hang very low and Bill, being rather tall, had to watch out and not bang his head.

I started to meet quite frequently with Bob, my old friend and colleague from Uganda. He was working for a hotel group in Hong Kong in the designing department. Through his assistance, we heard of a number of hotel projects in China, which his company were not interested in. Before I could contact some of them I was asked to go to Tianjin as project manager for a company hotel under construction. Once a flight was secured, we telexed my time of arrival and request for accommodation. On arrival at Tianjin Airport, I could not find anyone waiting for me and as there were no other Westerners around, I felt more and more lost. Most of the taxis had already left.

Just when I was wondering what to do a young Chinese man approached me in English and asked me if he could assist. I told him my plight.

'If you wait another five minutes you won't find any transport to take you to town,' he said. 'Why not come with me? I have a taxi outside and I drop you at the number-one hotel.'

Glad to have somebody to take care of my problem, I accepted gladly. On the way to town, which was about twenty kilometres from the airport, my driver told me he was a tourist guide employed by the Chinese Tourist Office and had brought some clients to the airport to catch a plane to Peking. He dropped me outside the hotel, which did not give the impression of being number one in anything. Before my departure from Hong Kong, I got in touch with a contact I received from Bob and as they were in negotiation with the renovating and refurbishing of a downtown hotel in Tianjin, I arranged to meet him during my time there.

After I made the reception clerk, who spoke very little German, understand that I would like to phone the number of the company's office in town, there was no reply. So there was nothing else to do than book a room in this rundown hotel for the night. When asking for a room, the clerk led me to understand that the hotel was fully booked. What to do now? Maybe the contact from Hong Kong, who I was scheduled to meet in the next few days, was staying in this place. I was in luck and was shown to his room. He was sitting in his pyjamas on the bed, having a business discussion with a local Chinese man, who was sitting on the other bed drinking a whisky. I explained my problem.

'You could always sleep here in this bed, but unfortunately it is already occupied, but let me talk with the reception and see what can be done,' was his reply. 'You just wait here and have a drink,' he said after putting down the phone.

After a few minutes, the phone rang and a short discussion on the phone ensued. Then it turned out that the manager had agreed to put a camp bed in the main office for the night, but that I had to vacate by 6.30 a.m. So I slept between antique typewriters and old-fashioned desks. A bathroom was next door and before retiring I had a shower. Just as well as by 6 a.m. there was a great commotion, throat clearing and gargling coming from the bathroom, where the clerks had arrived to commence their work. I got dressed quickly and disappeared to have a walk before breakfast was served. Already there were a lot of people on the road, going to work either on foot, on their bicycles or by bus.

During the course of the morning, I contacted the company successfully and by midday the chief engineer arrived at the hotel to join me for lunch. There was on offer a small, Western-style à la carte menu, but on advice from my colleague we ate Chinese. During the course of the meal, he informed me that he would try to book accommodation at the Chinese-owned Grand Hotel, just outside the city centre, and let me know later if he could obtain a room there but for tonight I'd better stay here. This time I was given a large room with a bathroom. The room must have seen better times and the furniture was old and cheap, not to mention the bed. I think I have never slept so badly as on this particular night. The mattress was very thin and the support underneath full of holes. Every time I turned, I dropped through another hole.

The next day I received confirmation of a room at the Grand Hotel and the company car arrived later to take me there. The driver, to my surprise, spoke a little English and he pointed out various landmarks on the way there. Apparently, he explained, because the company did not have a telex of their own, they used the machine at the Friendship Hotel and collected messages every day late in the afternoon. Therefore they did not know of my arrival until one hour after my plane landed at the airport. They sent the driver straightaway but by that time I had already left.

Chapter Fifteen

My new home, situated in a large park, consisted of two large complexes, each with 300 rooms with an impressive forecourt, dominated by a large fountain and a drive-in and parking area for around 150 cars, although I seldom saw more than ten cars parked at any time. In the entrance lobby there was the reception, the bank, with a corridor leading to the dining room on one side, a post office and telex room with a small bar that was never open and a corridor leading to some office and meeting rooms. On the first floor was a Friendship shop where one could buy souvenirs, local jewellery and imported liquor. My room was on the first floor, reachable by two lifts. In every Chinese hotel I had seen so far, there was a concierge or floor porter, with a desk on every floor. Here you deposit your key, daily departures, hand in your washing to be laundered and obtain information, which was always difficult, as the staff did not speak any foreign language.

I used to send my laundry every three or four days for cleaning. The cost for laundering was ridiculously low. The pressing left much to be desired and the cleaned items were handed back fastened together with string. Dry cleaning took two to three days, which was relatively short, as I was told by a Chinese man that he had to wait at least one month for his. I also remember reading an advertisement in the English-language daily that one Mr Ju opened a new dry-cleaning business and guaranteed a waiting time not longer than six weeks.

Also it was the first time that I've seen trousers returned from cleaning longer than before; usually they shrink. One day while collecting my laundry, for which you pay cash on the spot, I discovered an extra item on the bill. When I asked what this charge represented, I was told that they cleaned the linen-washing bag, in which the daily clothing was placed to be washed.

In the mornings, the company driver collected me, but in the evenings I often walked from the site to the hotel, passing a bicycle parking house on the way where several hundred were parked for about half a cent per day. There were always a number of horse-drawn wagons on the road, drawn by two or more horses. Each one had a square wooden frame covered on his behind to catch the droppings as this was collected for manure for the gardens.

The restaurant at the hotel consisted of three rooms, seating around fifty persons each, much too small for the size of the hotel, especially during dinnertime. You had to queue or share a table with other diners, mostly Chinese. Many times one or two rooms were occupied by private parties, so the waiting time grew longer. By 8.30 p.m. the restaurant closed and if you did not have a place it was your bad luck and you had to go hungry or hire a taxi to take you to one of the downtown restaurants, of which there were plenty, only serving Chinese food.

If you were alone, the only thing was to purchase a few biscuits at the Friendship shop and make yourself a cup of tea in your room. For this purpose each room was provided with a two-litre thermos flask in which hot water was changed twice a day, a cup with a lid and some tea bags with China tea. The idea was to place the tea into the cup, pour hot water over it, and cover and leave it for a time. If the water was sufficiently hot, you were all right; otherwise all the coarser pieces of tea would float on the top, which made it quite difficult to drink the brew.

In the restaurant you were served a very limited choice of European food, which was quite unpalatable, so most of the time you ordered Chinese food. You watched what other people were served and if it looked good, you pointed to the dish and asked the waitress to bring you the same.

There were three Scandinavian airline communication engineers staying at the hotel and an American science professor at the same time. Generally we had dinner together. One of our pastimes, while we waited for our order to arrive, was to try to pick up three peanuts in a line with the chopsticks. On many occasions the wrong food was served and trying to explain to the waitress about it was a waste of time.

Some days you ended up ordering two breakfasts because, as you entered the restaurant, a waitress came along to take your order. Tea or coffee with toast (with butter or marmalade) was the normal request, maybe together with scrambled or fried egg. Once you had given your order, you settled back to await your food. Don't ask me why, but it always took about ten or fifteen minutes before one item arrived. Most likely coffee and toast, then another five minutes for butter and jam and another ten minutes for the remainder. Anyway, as you were waiting, getting impatient, another waitress would come along for you to order. In the beginning I would try to explain that I had already ordered, but without success, and to have my peace, first thing in the morning, I would order a second time. By the time it usually arrived, I was already on my way to work.

Our hotel, under construction, was situated in an area surrounded by small lakes and right next to the old English club, of which all the old buildings were still standing. The place looked drab, the water in the swimming pool was dirty and definitely not an invitation to swim.

Our offices were installed in a building that must also have belonged to the club. The first floor was the sleeping and eating area for some of the expatriate engineers. I must say, they did not really live in great comfort and the air was always stuffy: cold in the winter, hot in the summer. The water supply was frequently cut off because the town was often short of this commodity and they had to go two or three days without. They cooked their own food and, being Singaporeans, their food varied somewhat from the local cuisine.

However, to break the monotony, we frequently went out to sample the fare in local restaurants. If you were hygiene-minded, you'd better stay at home. A Western health inspector would have a heart attack if he ever entered some of these places, but if there was nothing else available, you had to eat if you did not want to starve. I have a broad mind and can overlook most things, but when people spit all over the place, accompanied with a lot of coughing while you are trying to eat, then my stomach nearly turns over.

To train some of the staff in hotel catering and service, the company was running a restaurant in town in a large new complex of about thirty or forty restaurants and an equal number of takeaways. Apparently the mayor of the town visited the USA some years ago and was very impressed by Western food streets, which made him decide to build something similar in Tianjin. So this large building was built, but important things were left out and one was the toilets. Where the people went to relieve themselves of nature's call remains a mystery, Although this great square complex was only completed six months before it was now dirty and unhygienic, with empty crates all over the place, dustbins overflowing, and looked more like a hundred years old.

Like everywhere else in China, the bicycle was the main transport and also to a certain extent the fastest. The Scandinavian engineers brought along with them two made in Sweden and on a Sunday afternoon I used to borrow a bike from them and we set off about town to visit the department stores. Many times we were the cause of small accidents because the Chinese, never having seen a modern Western bicycle, forgot to look where they were driving and collided with other cyclists.

If you think you have experienced a crowd during Christmas in Oxford Street in London, you haven't seen anything like here in China. Masses of people push and shove you along. The space between the counters is packed like the London underground during rush hours. How anyone could purchase something in peace was beyond me. All the goods were locally manufactured and I must say the choice and quantity was better than I expected. To be able to control the crowds, no motorcar or bike was allowed to enter the area. You had to leave your transport in a parking lot, supervised and guarded by the town's controller. Usually there was a large crowd admiring my friends' bikes when we returned.

Tianjin is a large harbour town and it is only a two-hour train ride from Peking. It is the main port for the capital. Although you would still see the Western influence when driving through the town, it has lost most of it through the Cultural Revolution.

There are, though, still the German houses built and designed by German architects, the French section with houses which you still come across in the old parts of many French cities, and of course the English houses. I could well imagine what it must have looked like with well-tended gardens in front of the houses, and the sound of foreign languages. Nothing of all this remained except the buildings, which were in need of attention.

I was asked by the University of Tianjin to give a number of lectures to their students in the department of hotel management, which was only recently formed, but as I was shortly to leave for Hong Kong, I was not able to oblige, though I would have been happy to help them.

Tianjin is not only a large harbour town, it is also the fourth largest city in China, with considerable industry, both light and heavy. The factories employ thousands of people and conditions were about the same as around the end of the nineteenth century in Europe. They were covered with soot and dust from the black smoke of the chimneys and the dust caused by the workings.

The government had built enormous housing blocks that housed about 200 to 300 families each. Hot water was not available and the electricity supply was erratic most of the time. Some factories worked on Sundays to spread the consumption. During my stay, I also visited some modern factories, which were established under a joint venture scheme with a Western concern. They worked with modern machinery and were semi-automatic. The management was mostly Chinese with European experts to ensure good standard of production.

On three or four occasions I was requested to attend meetings in Peking. The express train from Tianjin took about two hours and travelled about one hundred to 120 kilometres per hour, drawn by an electric engine.

Two classes were available: hard seats and soft seats; business people and most Westerners took soft seats. The seats were covered with a white cloth and tea was available, each car having its own attendant. Arriving in Peking station was an experience in itself. The staircases and corridors leading from the platform to the forecourts of the station were so heavily occupied, you were cramped like sardines. To fall over was impossible; you were just pushed and shoved until you were outside the station. To obtain a ticket was just as cumbersome and I only attempted it once and after that I usually sent the company messenger, but each time he required my passport otherwise a ticket would not be issued.

During my stay I also visited the hotel that was to be modernised and refurbished as mentioned earlier on.

I took with me a Chinese-speaking engineer and went there about 9 a.m. The hotel, situated in the old French section, was quite impressive from the outside. But what a mess inside! The manager we found in his office with three other persons, smoking and drinking tea. We were invited to have some tea and, after explaining the purpose of our visit, we were taken around the hotel by a member of the staff, first to the first floor where the stale human smell was really overpowering. Each room had as many beds as possible; in certain cases you had to step over beds to reach your own allocated bed. Everywhere were spittoons. Some toilets were working somehow, while others were broken. When asked the price of a bed, I was told in the region of about five to ten cents. Occupancy, apparently, was very high throughout the year. Funnily enough there were some suites available which were somewhat better equipped, but the bathrooms had paint peeling off the walls and the bathtub and toilets were rust coloured.

The last straw was the kitchens, if one could call them that. I thought that the best way to bring this place up to date would be to demolish the whole of the interior and start from scratch, leaving the outside, as it was, as I mentioned before, quite impressive. This was exactly what the architect had in mind, I found out when I met him on my return to Hong Kong.

Back in Hong Kong, I started to pursue some other projects and as Bill was away in the USA, it was up to me to start the ball rolling. Bob informed me of a project in Zhaoqing where a Chinese company wanted to modernise a hotel and were also looking for management for their second unit. Zhaoqing is about eighty kilometres from Canton or Guangzhou as it is called today. The hotels were situated in a national park with a number of small lakes and crags, a small version of the lakes and crags in Guilin. To get there you could take the train to Guangzhou (Canton) and from there travel by car or the riverboat that leaves Hong Kong every other night and arrives at about 9 a.m. the next day in Zhaoqing at the river harbour.

The first trip was with Bob, another executive from his company and a Hong Kong Chinese man named KJ who was born in Zhaoqing and had some very good contacts in the provincial government. Taking a taxi to the harbour, we had to queue outside the department building with about another 200 people, mostly Chinese peasants returning home with plenty of boxes and baskets. After passing, we boarded a ferry, which took us out to the harbour, where our ship was waiting. On arrival on the ship, KJ left us to go straight to the dining room to claim a table and wait for us after we had installed ourselves in our cabins. The reason for this was that the dining room was much too small to accommodate all the guests and a long waiting time was on the cards if you didn't grab a table on boarding the ship. Luckily, I had a cabin on my own on the upper deck.

I found the others already enjoying a beer when I joined them in the dining room. It seemed this room hadn't seen a paintbrush for a number of years. There were no proper chairs and the tablecloth must have been changed the last time some weeks before. You didn't need a menu; you could actually read from the tablecloth. Anyway, I had been through worse and I sat down with the others to quite a good meal. The place was full, the air hot and thick with cigarette smoke. People were already standing around the various tables to force you to leave as soon as you finished the meal. After about twenty-four tins of beer, we retired to the open deck and watched the coast passing by. The lights of Hong Kong illuminated the sky for many miles around. The TV showed a Chinese kung fu film, which was very much appreciated by the Chinese. We were the only expatriates apart from three American students on the boat. As night closed in and the lights of Hong Kong faded away, we called it quits and retired to our cabins. After a quite restful night, I got up about 7 a.m. and had a shave and a shower, if you could call it that. I suppose it fulfilled its purpose as I felt at least refreshed, but the shower cap was missing, the stone floor slippery and the water a brownish colour.

After coffee and some biscuits for breakfast, we watched the riverboats passing by. They were all shapes and sizes, some very fragile with motors about to give up. Some were so heavily loaded that water washed over the deck. The land on both sides was quite fertile and occasionally you saw some buffalo pulling a cart along the river. The water of the river was very muddy but that didn't stop some youngster taking a bath and waving at us.

About 9 a.m. the harbour building of Zhaoqing came in sight, surrounded by some old houses. The people were eager to get off the boat and even with all their boxes, crates, baskets and so on it didn't take long. We waited until nearly everybody had disembarked and then joined the long queue in front of the customs. We weren't long there when a Chinese customs officer came along, welcomed us to China and Zhaoqing, invited us to tea in the lounge, handed over our passports to be stamped without delay, had our luggage collected and wished us a good day. Outside we were met by a delegation of high provincial officers and were taken on a small tour of the town before arriving at our hotel, which was the older of the two. We were accommodated in the older section because the other hotel was fully booked. After we had been shown to our rooms and had a wash and freshening up, we met for a get-together.

The hotel is situated in a national park with splendid views over the green and lush countryside surrounded by crags and lakes. Like so many other Chinese-run hotels I have seen, the hotel was totally neglected. The splendid staircase leading to the hotel was overgrown with weeds and some of the steps were broken. To flush the toilet in my room, I was provided with a plastic bucket and to fill my bath took about fifteen minutes. Although there was a shower available, it didn't work and if it had been operational, I could not have used it as the shower curtain was missing. The restaurant was cold and damp, but the food, I must say, was quite good.

After our planning meeting we adjourned for lunch, which turned out to be quite a jolly affair as the three bottles of brandy we brought along as a present were consumed in no time. The driver who was to drive us around in the afternoon drank three glasses of neat brandy. We looked at each other and were thinking the same thing, but the trip around the national park and to the hotel finished without incident. Just below the hotel were a number of restaurants for the local visitors and we were told that one of them specialised in game. What game? we wanted to know.

Oh, snakes, other reptiles and dogs, we were told in reply. We decided to give this particular place a miss if we were going to be invited out.

The park was very nicely laid out with pergolas all around the lakes, inviting you to relax. Neat stone bridges criss-crossed the narrow parts of the lake. An artist centre sold genuine and antique Chinese art. Flowers and flowering bushes made the whole area very attractive. Mostly all the crags had small pagodas on the top, which could be reached on steep footpaths. Everywhere you could see Chinese inscriptions on the rock faces, which date back hundreds of years and had been restored in the last few years to their original state.

The hotel that we visited in the latter part of the afternoon was a very modern construction with a number of modern features. For example, it boasted two restaurants, one Chinese and one Western, which served Western food, a coffee shop and a disco to accommodate 600 persons.

The equipment was some of the latest on the market, but although only installed about six months ago, it was already in need of repair.

On the lower floor there was a complete shopping arcade selling local jewellery, handicrafts, radios, televisions, cameras, fridges and motorbikes manufactured in Japan. 'Why motorbikes?' I asked, as all goods purchased had to be paid for with tourist currency and the local Chinese were not, or were not supposed to be, in possession of this kind of money. 'We know how to get hold of this special currency,' was the reply. I also found a large supermarket within the arcade. As a hotelier I could not understand why they would have a supermarket available for tourists. Surely, it seems to me, it is cutting your own throat to invite guests to buy food at a shop to consume in their rooms.

On the lakeshore right next to the hotel you could hire small boats, enjoy waterskiing or, for a small fee, take a motorboat for a trip around the lake. If everything had been properly taken care of, some urgent maintenance carried out, the lake cleared of rubbish and the gardens looked after, you could have imagined yourself to be somewhere in Austria or Switzerland.

The residents of the hotel were mostly teenagers from Hong

Kong, free and easy in their behaviour. By mistake we were shown a bedroom that was occupied and the occupants were in the course of making love.

During dinner, one of the Chinese suggested we climb one of the nearest crags at 6 a.m. to give us a good appetite for breakfast, the next morning. Only one of our party took up the offer.

The next morning we were taken to the site of the proposed golf course. On the way we passed small rice fields where the local farmers and their water buffaloes were hard at work. It was getting hotter by the minute and I was really glad after the one-hour walkabout to be back again at the hotel for a cool beer. In the afternoon we resumed more discussions and agreed to sign a letter of intent the next day.

We were to provide the finance for the whole reconstruction of the hotel and for maintenance work at the hotel to the sum of five million dollars, and nine million dollars for the golf course. The Chinese would provide the labour and prepare the land for the new building and so on.

We were told right on our arrival that Zhaoqing was to be developed as a tourist centre to attract tourists from Hong Kong, Macau and as far as Japan, and to that effect they had started a small version of Disneyland, of which about twenty units were completed and already open to the public. Of course, we were eager to visit the site and it was decided that we would go there in the course of the evening and have dinner in one of the various restaurants. Although a 'small version of Disneyland' was a little too far-fetched a description, nevertheless the site could be favourably described as a pleasure garden similar to the Tivoli in Copenhagen or the Prater in Vienna.

Naturally they wanted us to try to participate in every attraction and I must confess we were really flaked out afterwards and were thankful to sit down for dinner. This time we were taken to a Western restaurant where we enjoyed a really first-class steak with fried potatoes and salad, followed by ice cream and fresh fruit. The service was excellent and when I enquired where the staff had acquired their skills, I was told the manager was especially recruited from Hong Kong for this purpose.

Having achieved what we came for, we booked our passage

back to Hong Kong, but the boat was not leaving for another day. It was suggested that we take a ride into the nearby mountains. The journey took us about one hour, and it was pleasantly cool and really enjoyable. We were dropped near a Buddhist temple and were welcomed with tea by the head monk. Later on we were joined by the temple director, which according to Chinese law is a layman that is not a monk but someone employed and paid for by the government to administrate the temple. The tea we were served was made from a local herb collected each spring by the monks, dried, packed and sold in the towns. The temple, its buildings and so on were on the whole very primitive and we were allowed to watch a religious ceremony. In the kitchen we were shown an enormous wok, where apparently food was prepared for over 500 pilgrims who visited the temple during religious festivals. Having said goodbye to our host, we descended on foot down the mountainside through small valleys and steep stairs, passing a pool at the bottom of a waterfall where people were enjoying a cool and refreshing swim. Pity we did not have any swimming trunks with us as otherwise we could have joined them, because by now we were wet through from the humidity in the air.

By 3 p.m. we were back at the hotel and we were told to be ready at 6 p.m. for a farewell dinner at a good Chinese restaurant just outside the national park. The meal was first class and consisted of eight courses. Because I had mentioned some days earlier that I liked garlic, one of the dishes of braised pork was cooked with a lot of garlic bulbs and I was obliged to eat about half of them.

We all enjoyed the meal tremendously, although we did not know what we were served. To answer our questions we were told that one dish was steamed snake steaks, the others buffalo, sea lion, pork, river fish and wild dog. I think if some of us had known the menu in advance, it would not have been enjoyed so much.

On our boat trip back to Hong Kong, I reflected on the visit. One thing I noticed was that we were never left on our own, that we always had someone taking care of us. Secondly the government official never paid for the meals at the various restaurants and that they were always treated with great respect wherever we went. I made enquiries about this on my later visits and it was explained to me that a government official, even if he occupies a high position, is paid a relatively small salary but that he enjoys certain privileges, such as free entertainment, the use of government transport and the permission to purchase certain imported goods. This probably explains the reason why they always ate each meal with us: free food and drink.

I woke early in the morning because the humming of the engines had stopped. I was afraid that one engine had broken down but when I looked out of the porthole I noticed we had arrived in Hong Kong. We were lying there for about two hours before the ferry arrived to take us ashore. By now, Bill had returned from the States and concentrated on drawing and designing proposed alterations for the hotel.

At the same time, we contacted various financial houses and banks for the funding of the enterprise and instructed a competent firm to prepare a financial estimate and determine the feasibility of the project. Within a few weeks we had the estimated funds available, but now the Bank of China started dragging their feet with granting the guarantee and in addition the whole enterprise suddenly needed approval from higher authorities in China. I should have expected this, as I had already had the same experience in Tianjin when we negotiated a hotel project in the north of China, and another one in Xian.

Every time you thought that everything was now signed and sealed, there was always another obstacle to be overcome.

In the next few months, we made additional visits to Zhaoqing and were always welcomed with open arms, but the negotiations had become bogged down due to the slowness of government offices. We were assured that everything would be all right in the end, but things could not be rushed and had to take their time. By then we were involved in another project, a hotel with 300 rooms and apartments and office buildings in Shanghai. In this case, all the plans were ready, but the Chinese owner was too greedy and demanded ten per cent commission of the building costs. So that was the end of that. To top everything, the company I was working for had financial difficulties and the banks were reluctant to provide further funds. Funding stopped completely for the Tianjin project and all but two expatriate engineers were withdrawn. Bill decided to form his own company with backing from American businessmen and it was decided to concentrate fully on that.

Chapter Sixteen

Morocco

After my return from Hong Kong and China, it was nice to see Mavis, my son and my family again after such a long time.

Now a search for a new assignment started all over again. Having spent nearly all the winter at home, an offer to be general manager of a group of hotels at Agadir in Morocco came along. In total there were five hotels involved, with a total of 2,500 beds, catering for mass tourism. The newest hotel had just opened its doors and was not quite complete as such facilities as the night-club, tennis courts and a second swimming pool were not expected to be finished for another nine months, but the things completed looked attractive and welcoming. So the following March, in 1986, Mavis and I packed our suitcases again and were off to another part of the world.

We settled in our apartment in town and I got down to the serious business of getting the hotels organised. It was not always easy as money for badly needed equipment was not exactly forthcoming, although the hotels were profitable.

Mass tourism was something new to me and needed quite some adjusting on my part. I did spend a lot of time at the hotels in order to learn at first hand the ins and outs of mass tourism. I must confess that it was quite an experience.

The first problem mostly started at the reception after the check-in of a planeload of holidaymakers. Some of them wanted to change their rooms, because they did not face the sea or did not get enough sun; others wanted a room not near the pool or further up, with balcony or with a small garden in the front.

I need not say that I did feel sorry for the poor receptionist, having to deal with sometimes quite rude and in my opinion unreasonable and demanding guests.

The biggest problem we faced at the newest unit was that the second dining room was a long way from completion and we had therefore only seating capacity for around half of the guests staying at the hotel. To cope with this situation, we had to close the entrance doors once all the seats were taken. This resulted in the situation that about fifteen minutes before dinner there was a long queue forming outside the entrance and there were many complaints from the people who could not be accommodated waiting outside, for at least another half hour until their turn came.

Having to cater for so many different nationalities was another headache we were confronted with. For the Italians, there was never enough pasta on the menu; for the English the tea tasted of dishwater; while the Germans wanted more heavy and starchy food. Our breakfast consisted of a continental breakfast, with such additional items as fresh fruit and fruit juices. Roughly sixty per cent of our guests were on half-pension, so they collected enough bread, rolls, butter, jam and fresh fruit to provide them with sufficient supplies for a lunch, which they promptly proceeded to eat at the pool terrace and snack bar, with the cheek to ask the waiter to bring them a glass of iced water. We had no other choice than to make a charge for anyone caught taking food from the dining room.

Salaries paid to the staff were very low and I still wonder today how someone making so little money was able to pay for accommodation and in many cases support a family on top of it. Not surprisingly pilfering was rife, and measures to prevent pilfering were high on our list of priorities. Strangely enough, very little was stolen from the guests, but the hotel's small equipment found its way to the local market, where there were always buyers to be found.

Here is a typical example. Tablemats were made from paper in use for the restaurant. Table linen would have been too expensive and the cost of having them laundered too high. One member of the staff started collecting them after every meal as they were discarded, smoothed the mats out and sold them to a merchant in the souk.

As it happened, local shop owners went there to buy packing paper for their goods. I remember once buying a small loaf of bread that was packed in a page of a discarded Bible. Anyway, these tablemats must have been bought by a butcher from whom the managing director and chairman's wife bought her meat. She was therefore very surprised to find the meat wrapped in one of the hotel's paper mats.

Life was very inexpensive and for very little money you could enjoy a good meal with a bottle of local wine. Once you found your way around, it was easy to find which restaurants catered for the tourists as the prices were higher than in other places.

We used to spend many an hour at the souk. One never became tired of wandering among the stalls and looking at all the many things on display.

I am sure one could find whatever one wished if one searched long enough. There were the sections that sold souvenirs – carpets and so on – for the tourists, and there was the fruit and vegetable market where local goods were always available in great quantities and at very low prices.

The goods were mostly just thrown on the ground and you picked out for yourself what you wanted. Particularly fascinating was the meat section, where live chickens were sold, killed, plucked and put in a plastic bag and you went away with your Sunday lunch ready for cooking.

There was another section where tourists very seldom ventured, but I found it quite absorbing, looking at about everything on offer somebody could want. Broken furniture, radios, used and often broken tools, rusted nails; as I said, just about everything a poor person needed for a few dinars. You could have your shoes soled with a piece of a car tyre. For a few cents you received a haircut. Shacks with a paraffin stove sold local food at throwaway prices.

Chapter Seventeen

Egypt

At the beginning of October 1991 at 10 a.m. the director of the hotel school in Passug asked me if I would like to go to Egypt to instruct hotel staff in the food and beverage department for a period of approximately two months. He wanted my decision by midday. I phoned Mavis and she had no objection; probably she knew that hotel management was more to my liking than teaching at the school. So I gave my consent and was told to be ready to travel within the next two or three days; also if I wanted to take my wife along there would be no objection. However, Mavis decided to stay at home as we had, as she rightly said, dug ourselves in. So 10 October 1991 found me flying off to Cairo, where I was met by a company executive and taken to the Moevenpick Hotel for the night. The next day I met with the chairman, after a small introduction of the company's organisation, which operated at that moment two hotels with a third nearing completion, sixteen buses for round trips, one hotel ship on the Nile, three travel agents plus a purchasing and supply set-up.

Then arrived the point of my personal involvement as a teacher within the organisation. It came somewhat as a surprise when I was asked to take over the management of the run-down three-star hotel, which was redecorated and refurnished, situated near the pyramids. Somewhere along the line there must have been a communication breakdown, but it did not worry me too much if I was teaching or managing. In a certain way, the latter was more appealing to me.

Around midday the local executive, who was to spend some time with me, drove us to the hotel.

The refurbishing and some of the renovation was complete, with the exception of some bedrooms.

At this stage, it is important to say something about the hotel's amenities, which consisted of seventy-four double rooms with bed, a separate toilet, TV and telephone. Six suites were available for guest accommodation. There was a coffee shop on the ground floor, a restaurant and an Arabian coffee house on the first floor with a disco in the basement and a nightclub on the eighth floor, plus two souvenir shops, a hotel lobby with reception-cashier desk and a bank for foreign exchange, as well as a bar.

The kitchen area was very large and seemed to be stocked with all necessary equipment. In addition the hotel had its own laundry and sufficient storage rooms. There were around eighty staff on the payroll.

The public rooms were pleasantly decorated and I was quite impressed with the general appearance until I asked to see the back areas of the hotel. I have seen messy and dirty places, but what confronted me here was the pits. Every corner was a dumping place for rubbish and the fire escape was blocked with items of every description.

Mavis decided to join me after all but there was not really much to do during the day apart from visiting the pyramids, walking around the neighbourhood markets and doing a little shopping. She did a bit of typing for me, as I did not have a secretary at the time. We used to go for small strolls on a Friday, the official weekly holiday. The hotel adjoined the main trunk road to Alexandria with six traffic lanes. Apart from between 3 a.m. and 6 a.m. in the morning, the traffic was so heavy it was suicide to attempt to cross the road. No vehicle was prepared to stop for anyone to pass and the traffic cops were more interested in directing the traffic than paying attention to pedestrians. Crossing the road meant first watching for a chance to cross, then making a dash to reach the other side.

Staff morale was at its lowest. Nobody seemed to show any interest, and just sat around killing time. So for about three days, I just walked around taking notes, formalising decisions for the future.

The first action was to call a staff meeting. I must say I was not very complimentary in my introduction and made it quite clear to all of them that drastic changes would take place without delay.

Anybody not agreeing with the new turnaround was entitled to quit. On the other hand, I promised to raise the salaries of the deserving and good staff. I think a word on salaries paid in Egypt at this moment is quite appropriate. According to the payroll, some junior staff were paid approximately forty Swiss francs per month with meals during working hours so it was not surprising the staff were uninterested in their work, uncooperative and unmotivated.

Next in line were the heads of departments. There I was franker and demanded a complete change in their attitude, fullest implementation of decisions and cooperation between departments.

Within the next few days the first heads started to roll. By the end of the first month, out of the twelve heads of departments, only three remained. Fortunately, with the help of company executives, I was able to find competent replacements within a relatively short time and the standard of the hotel started to improve every day. I must confess, the first few weeks were sheer hell. Without a proper back-up team, everything fell on my shoulders. Simple decisions were referred to me any time during the day or night.

As the hotel was ninety per cent involved in group business, staying an average of one and a half days, a lot was demanded from the staff. It could happen that one group departed at midnight and the next arrived at 3 a.m. So the rooms had to be cleaned and the linen changed in relatively short times, and this in the middle of the night. All this would have been a somewhat easy problem but unfortunately the hotel was desperate for linen. An order for new linen had been placed some time ago and delivery was expected shortly. When it finally arrived, though, sheets were found to have no hem at the top and bottom so they had to go back to the factory.

As already mentioned beforehand, the kitchen seemed fully equipped, but to my surprise, only about sixty per cent was in working order. I ordered the chief engineer to introduce a twenty-four-hour shift and to seek the help of an outside contractor to carry out the required repairs.

The chef was very uncooperative to start with, but suddenly became fully involved, taking full control and motivating his cooks.

Luckily, I did not have to terminate directly any member of staff myself, which could have involved the company in unnecessary court cases. Instead I started initiating a plan, criticising or plain hammering the person I wanted to leave until they had had enough or could not stand anymore and just resigned. However, the one person who could not be persuaded to resign was the head receptionist. To a certain extent it exhausted my patience sometimes, because she took any criticism without the slightest concern.

All the new executives entrenched themselves as a team, started making decisions on their own and were fully committed to their job and the training of staff.

And throughout all this, healthwise I felt on top of the world and I did enjoy my work.

Near the end of my engagement, when the chairman informed me that the school had extended my secondment until the beginning of the new semester 1992, which meant that I would not be back home until mid-January 1992. I requested four days' leave, as I had not had any days off since my arrival in Cairo, and I wished to go back to Switzerland and travel back with Mavis.

Back home we started to inform everyone concerned of our intended absence and I had a request to visit the school, to discuss one or two details. Not expecting anything, we found a red-carpet welcome awaiting us, with a special lunch together with all the students and a present for my sixty-fifth birthday. I must say I was very touched by all the arrangements insofar as Mavis and I had a birthday party planned and booked for about twenty people on 23 October 1991. The invitations had already been mailed, but everything had to be cancelled due to my departure for Egypt.

On 10 November, we arrived back in Cairo. By now my shadow (the company executive) had been replaced by a young, keen and ambitious man without any previous hotel experience, but with tour-leader qualifications. During the remaining few weeks in Cairo I took him under my wing to teach him as much as possible in the short time remaining, as he showed good potential for becoming a hotel manager.

The nightclub on the eighth floor did not come under the

jurisdiction of the hotel management as it was leased by the owning company, chiefly because they were in financial difficulties and hoped to offset some of the expenses by leasing out the club premises.

The reputation of the club left much to be desired and as far as the hotel was concerned caused us numerous complaints. The music played was so loud that guests on the seventh and sixth floors were unable to sleep soundly. The patrons frequenting the club were definitely not the people the hotel wanted to see on its premises. The last were always seen leaving around 7 a.m. and caused quite a stir among the early tourists. The girls, mostly prostitutes in miniskirts and heavy make-up, were not a nice sight in the early morning hours. Repeated complaints by management had little or no effect. The contract signed unfortunately left no real loophole to terminate the arrangement.

Although quite a lot of loose ends needed to be tied up, the hotel was picking up good advance bookings for the coming high season.

The word must have got around the travel and tour operators regarding the changes at the hotel and they were keen to book their groups with us. For ten US dollars for bed and breakfast, private bath, telephone, minibars and TV, I was not surprised that they all wanted to conduct business with us. Amir, my shadow, had considerable experience in the tour business and had really good contacts, so I could leave that side of the operation entirely to him. By now an experienced food and beverage specialist had joined the organisation and together we designed the menus and à la carte for the hotel. Egyptian laws and regulations for the hotel and catering industry are quite complicated and I was also depending on him a lot in this respect.

I think I had never put on weight so fast in the past, chiefly because the food and beverage executive insisted that I taste every dish before it was included on the à la carte menu.

We were lucky to find a first-class baker and pastry cook and the fresh croissant rolls and Danish pastries every morning were another temptation to forget my diet and eat what was to me forbidden food due to my heart condition.

In addition we offered a takeaway of cakes and petit fours, so that a piece of cake usually accompanied the morning and afternoon coffee.

The maintenance department still remained a headache. The man in charge, although a very good all-rounder, lacked leadership skills, and was just not able to supervise and organise the department. So it was left to me and my assistant to chase around and see that things were done.

The hotels in Egypt, I found, were all very security-conscious and as the previous security supervisor had given notice, I was looking for a very competent and experienced candidate. The company chairman offered his good services to find the right man for me. He insisted that the person he had in mind should be a retired army or police officer, as according to his explanation, the man would have had to deal with various government offices in regard to labour problems, licences, court cases and so on and therefore his contacts could be beneficial to the hotel in solving problems.

I personally wanted a more down-to-earth person with police experience to lead this section and leave the labour problems to the personnel department to deal with, licences to the chief accountant and court cases to the company lawyers. My arguments did not convince sufficiently and I was waiting to meet his candidates. So the first one arrived one morning, a former colonel in the army. Wearing dark sunglasses, white shirt and black suit, he looked like a member of the Mafia. The responsibilities involved in his job were explained to him, together with all other relevant information, to which he agreed without comment. Although I was confirmed in my own mind he was not able to carry out the duties satisfactorily, he was employed but failed to return after four working days.

Number two was a retired admiral, about sixty-eight years old. When he was shown his office, he requested easy chairs, a sofa, coffee tables and an executive desk for himself. Asked why all this elaborate furniture, his reply was that he would have to deal with very high officials during the course of his duties and wanted to impress them. Next he refused to eat in the restaurant with the other executives but wanted a table for himself, also choosing from the à la carte menu. When told that this would not be possible and was in contrast with the existing hotel regulations, he replied that he wished for similar privileges to the general manager. Naturally, I could not agree to his demands. Not to offend the hotel owner I did engage him but made it clear that he had to accept the hotel rules. For five days he sat all day in the hotel lobby, drinking coffee and tea, reading newspapers and having no intention of supervising the security department. Needless to say, I could not tolerate his attitude any longer and I terminated his employment.

By now I was under considerable stress and had to take more medication. One day I felt really bad and I asked my assistant to accompany me to the hospital for a check-up. The results were so bad that the doctors refused to allow me to return to the hotel and instead put me to bed in the intensive care unit. For the next three days I was examined continuously. Heart specialists from the Cairo university were consulted and nothing spared to help me to recover. Everyone was really great and could not do enough.

The last few days before leaving the hospital, I was in a suite with private bath and room service. To my astonishment the total bill amounted, in terms of Swiss francs, to 800 for ten days' treatment. Medical care and a hospital bed could have amounted to ten times more in Switzerland.

Before I had been taken ill, it had been decided that I should transfer to Aswan to assist opening the Hotel Basma, a new unit of the company due to open before the New Year.

So after my release from hospital and three days at the Pyramid, Mavis and I packed our cases and flew to Aswan.

Aswan

The hotel, supremely situated overlooking the Nile, was still a long way from completion. Although everybody worked hard to beat the deadlines, we were fighting a losing battle. We were able to accept some guests, but needless to say we did receive many complaints.

The company kindly offered Mavis a trip on the company riverboat for a Nile cruise to visit Luxor and other interesting sites along the route. To begin with, we were accommodated at the New Cataract Hotel, a five-star operation. The bedroom was spacious and well equipped but dreadfully cold at night as no heating was provided whatsoever. To make matters worse, the window frames were not airtight and even closing the curtains did not prevent the cold night air from entering the room. The food served was acceptable, but certainly not five star. Due to the approaching Christmas and New Year period, all the hotels in Aswan were fully booked and overbooked to such an extent that Cataract Hotels moored a floating hotel on the riverbank adjoining the hotel grounds to accommodate the overflow. Our rooms were required and we moved to the Basma, where conditions were not quite as good as at the Cataract.

During a visit of the Egyptian hotel company chairman to Switzerland and the hotel school the previous summer, it had been agreed to offer some students the opportunity to work in the Egyptian company's various hotels during the Christmas break. Unfortunately the ones that were allocated to the Aswan hotel had a bit of a rough ride but were compensated by being taken around the historical sites around Aswan and Luxor, and entertained for Christmas and New Year dinner in a five-star hotel in Aswan. Agreed, they did expect something different when they accepted the offer for Egypt, but despite this, the experience gave them a good insight into a hotel opening that did not proceed according to normal circumstances. They learnt to accept the situation and to live with it.

With the chaotic overbooking situation in all hotels in Aswan, we had no chance to reserve rooms for guests who possessed confirmed bookings with us. With the limited facilities available in our hotel, we made their stay as comfortable as possible. At least they had heating in their rooms and the standard of the meals offered was high above the competition. The general manager of the hotel arrived just before Christmas and together with the help of head-office executives, we showed at least that we were capable of carrying and looking after our guests.

My secondment to Egypt drew to a close and on 15 January 1992 we left for Switzerland, where I reported back for my duties at the hotel school. Although I spent nearly four months altogether in Egypt, I saw very little of the country's wonderful and very interesting historical sites. The nearest view of the pyramids was from my office windows in Cairo at the hotel. One day I hope to visit and see for myself what I missed.

We started getting settled again in Lüen and although it was winter I found enough work in the house to keep me going, together with my lessons at the hotel school. Many fine afternoons found me cross-country skiing in Parpan. Alas, it was not long until the day when a further request arrived from Egypt to take over as general manager at the Basma hotel in Aswan. So there we were again, packing our cases and leaving Switzerland behind.

The hotel was now completed and enjoying good occupancy. March is usually a mild month and the guests were mostly sunbathing around the pool. Swimming was not very inviting, as the pool was not heated and the water too cold. To carry out the necessary maintenance work, we decided to empty the pool, as no one was swimming. Messages were posted in the hotel lobby and placed in every room to this effect. I knew from previous experience that some guests would certainly complain to the travel operator, and sure enough, there they were with their cameras, taking pictures of the empty pool and not long afterwards the complaints started arriving. I think that crowning all the complaints was the one from a German tourist asking for DM 800 compensation because he was disturbed by the police sirens accompanying the state president during his visit to Aswan.

The tourist season was at its height and the riverfront full of ships cruising between Aswan and Luxor. Then everything changed overnight. The fundamentalists attacked a town bus and shooting was taking place in downtown Aswan. The tourists stayed away and we found ourselves with 240 staff looking after twenty guests. The owners were not prepared to dismiss any of them and now a new chapter of hotel management faced me: how to keep such a large labour force busy. Once everybody caught up with their entitled holidays, the problems really started. The executives had their hands full to keep them going. I have never seen so much unnecessary cleaning going on. Our daily meeting consisted mainly of finding jobs for the staff to try to keep them in line.

Mavis and I strolled along the bazaar nearly every evening.

The shopkeepers got to know us, but that did not stop them trying to sell us their goods. The newspaper vendor, a young boy, hailed us as soon as we were spotted, even from across the road, to sell his papers. He also sold books and Mavis paid him a small fee to take them away and return again once read.

I started giving lessons to the staff, who were very keen to learn. I was also successful in obtaining some video films on hotel procedure, which they wished to see as often as possible. It is strange that with a hotel full of guests, the staff are fully occupied and do not have time to think of shortcomings and complaints. However, when there is time on their hands, the problems for management begin. We were bombarded with trifling complaints and special requests. We tried by holding regular meetings to reduce the situation. Do not make promises you cannot fulfil; otherwise there will be trouble.

As with all new large hotels, a grand opening is a must and Basma was no exception. The owners sent out invitations, including one to President Mubarak, which he accepted. Security police were all over the hotel, organising safety plans, and armed special snipers were stationed on the roof. All the personnel files of the staff were checked including all hotel residents. For the kitchens, it was a great challenge to prepare a buffet for about 400 persons, especially as this was something they had never experienced before. We engaged the services of a chef from a large Cairo hotel to assist and organise the buffet.

The President lodged in his own villa in Aswan and had a special programme to visit other various institutions in town. During the whole morning we could hear the police sirens around Aswan. Some of the hotel residents were alarmed but we informed them there was no reason to be afraid. As a firework display was planned, we needed permission from the provincial Governor. About two months before, another new hotel had an official opening and the governor informed me they had a display for half an hour. For our hotel he expected a display of at least three quarters of an hour, mostly because the President would be present.

The party went off without any problems and we were especially congratulated by the President.

Chapter Eighteen

Sharm el-Sheikh

In early September I received a phone call from the secretary of the Gazalla Hotel Company, which was also a partner and co-owner of the Basma Hotel, Aswan, asking if I was interested in taking over the management of the hotel. I consulted with the hotel school management, and they were prepared to release me for an unspecified period.

Accordingly I informed the Gazalla Hotel Company and agreed to travel towards the end of the month.

The hotel was situated next to the extensive beach on Naama Bay, had 320 beds divided between the two-storey main hotel building and rustic bungalows, grouped around two swimming pools. There was a poolside bar and adjacent to the promenade on the bay were the restaurant for the hotel guests, supplemented by a pizzeria, à la carte restaurant, two bars and a beachside disco with live music.

It was agreed that initially I should travel alone. I settled myself in quite cosily and as usual just observed the comings and goings around the hotel. The tourists seemed to be relaxed and happy.

The mainstream tourists arrived on a Saturday and I was amazed how efficiently the staff dealt with the departures and arrivals of the guests. The luggage handling was perfect. Within thirty minutes of the arrival of about 150 guests, the luggage was delivered to rooms. Interfering would have been unwise on my part.

The main restaurant offered breakfast and dinner buffets. For the sweet I favoured the chocolate ice cream and I had quite a job to convince the waiter not to bring me chocolate ice cream every day.

Most of the tourists were on half-pension; that is, breakfast and dinner. I observed quite a large number took items from the breakfast menu with them to eat later by the pool or on the beach. We printed notices for each table not forbidding the taking out of food, but informing them that a charge would be made accordingly. In the case of fresh fruit, we looked the other way.

Local wine was of a drinkable quality, and so both local and imported wine was offered. The government levied quite a heavy duty, especially on imported wine. Consequently the demand was very low. Local wine consumption was satisfactory and we wanted to increase the volume of sales. We offered the restaurant staff a small commission for the wine sold. This action did show some results. However, we had to issue additional information on the correct serving of wine, because to sell more wine, the glasses were filled right to the rim, with the result that if a party of five ordered a bottle of wine, there was not enough for the host so he was obliged to order an additional bottle.

The water was supplied by bowsers collected from a well about twenty kilometres from the hotel. The three large tanks at the hotel guaranteed sufficient water for the hotel's needs.

The guests were advised to buy purified water at a specially reduced price. The electrical wiring installed in the bungalows was of poor quality so when it rained, which fortunately was very seldom, the sparking from the wires was quite a sight. Between the two adjoining hotels a gully about twenty-five metres wide with stones and rocks separated the two buildings and with a wall one metre high along the edges of the gully. This was to channel floodwater to the sea and avoid damage to the hotels. You may ask from where the floods came. It happens that during the winter months it rains quite frequently in the hills of the hinterland. The water sweeps very rapidly towards the sea where the hotels are situated in the low-lying area of Naama, and so we could be very rapidly flooded. Near the maintenance section of the hotel, a large amount of sand was deposited which could be used to fill sandbags if needed.

The pizzeria, the only one on the bay, was very well frequented and a real profit-making unit. During lunch and evening time, people were queuing for a seat. The roof of the pavilion-style building was covered with brick-shaped wooden pieces. Unfortunately these slats were laid the wrong way and instead of the rainwater flowing directly to the roof channel, it was leaking through the roof on to the tables below. With umbrellas from the beach we were trying at least to have some dry space for guests. Fortunately it never rained for very long and if we dried the tables we were quickly in full swing.

On the beach itself and along the promenade, which was for cyclists and pedestrians, the Tam Tam bar was a favourite meeting place. It was constructed mainly from wood in a local style with matted floors and subdued lighting. The seating was palm trunks and water pipes were available on request if required. A few hundred metres away was the beach dancing club with live music and opposite the Tam Tam bar local specialities and fish dishes were served in an à la carte restaurant. On the terrace outside the restaurant one could observe carpet-makers at work. In all the areas of the hotel things were very lively.

The beaches of Naama Bay were privately owned by the various hotels. A few kilometres inland, the American army had a small base. The soldiers had no swimming facilities so we were approached by the commander asking if we would allow them to use our beach. I think we agreed to accommodate fifty on a daily basis. There were no real problems from the tourists and the girls were happy to have some company. The only problem was at night when the lads tried to visit the girls in their rooms. Our security staff had quite a problem keeping them out. Strict orders were issued against night visits to that effect but how can you prevent love-hungry soldiers from having a try.

One night a 'Night in the Desert' event was organised, with the cooperation of the local Bedouins. A suitable spot was agreed on for a year. The area was in a small valley and illuminated with petrol lights on either side. Tourists were asked to seat themselves on palm mats. Camels were available for rides and Arabian music was played by a local band.

The hotel provided a buffet of local specialities: grills, salads and sweets, plus refreshments. Twice, with the help of the owner, we were fortunate enough to obtain the Cairo Symphony Orchestra to perform a symphonic evening. Tickets were

143

available in various hotels and posters were displayed along the bay. Organisation of these events needed a great deal of work. Generators and loudspeakers had to be installed. The generators had to be quite a way from the site so that they did not interfere with the performance and the floodlights. All the requirements, such as plastic plates and cutlery, equipment for the buffet, food and beverages, needed careful planning. Anyway, the night was a great success.

I still had occasional heart problems. One morning it was rather bad and I asked one of my staff to drive me to the hospital for a check-up.

The hospital was an old wood building dating back to colonial times. Anyway, a young doctor in flip-flops and old trousers and shirt took care of me and guided me to a bedroom. He asked me to take off my clothes and to lie on the bed. In the time it took him to get the EKG unit, I had time to look around the room. The only furniture was the bed I lay on, a small bedside table and a naked electric bulb hanging from the ceiling, plus a few cockroaches running around the wall.

Eventually the doctor arrived with the unit but the electric cable had no plug so he inserted two wires into the socket and tried to switch it on but nothing happened. After trying a few times, he found out the fuse was gone. He checked my blood pressure and pulse, listened to my heart and came to the conclusion that there was really nothing wrong with me.

Fortunately there was a decompression station for divers in trouble in town. They agreed to perform check-ups and in case of emergency provide help.

The local meteorological service issued a possible flood warning in January. According to the report, heavy rain was expected in the mountains with flooding in the low laying areas. This meant that we could expect floodwater to reach Naama Bay. Usually it took about three days for the water to reach the sea after rain in the mountains.

Immediately we got ready, building a barrier of sand bags by the entrance to the hotel. The barrier was constructed in such a way that the floodwater was directed away from the hotel and would find its way to the specially constructed channels at each side of the hotel. The guests were informed of possible flooding and advised to place their belongings on the bed, chairs or table in the room. Each one was issued with a blanket in case they had to move to higher ground. Buses were hired to take them to safe areas.

Guests' records were removed from reception and stored on the first floor of the hotel block. These emergencies only applied to the bungalows. The two-storey hotel was safe. The kitchen was instructed to make arrangements to make packed lunches if required. It may be important to mention that the flood could subside rapidly and be over within an hour.

Luckily for us, the water, when it did arrive eventually, posed no danger to the property. Only slight damage was caused to the staff quarters, which were not protected. Only one of the neighbouring hotels had some minor flooding of their hotel buildings. Apparently the rainfall was not as heavy as expected in the inland areas and most of the water seeped away into the dessert.

With the hot summer weather approaching and the doctor's advice to avoid excessive high temperatures, a return to Lüen was advisable. Back at the hotel school I was promoted to school director and some months later mayor of Lüen.

Still with the desire to return to the hotel business, I registered with British Executive Services Overseas, an organisation providing developing countries with retired experts in various fields, including the hotel and catering industries. It did not take long until I received some interesting offers. One was in Oman assisting in a so-called food street, a complex housing various food outlets, but due to the hot climate I had to decline. Another was in China in a provincial town to put together and advise the future management teams. I discussed the proposal with my doctor and was made aware of the lack of proper facilities in case of a serious emergency. The third case was in Ecuador, to improve the infrastructure of a mountain resort hotel about 2,000 metres over sea level, but the height was too great for me.

After two years as school director and four years as village mayor, I said goodbye to all assignments and retired to my home.

Made in the USA
Las Vegas, NV
22 April 2022